David May
21/4/2008.
0868150325

D1614619

POEMS
1930–1989

with previously unpublished
poetry and translations

POEMS
1930–1989

SAMUEL BECKETT

CALDER PUBLICATIONS
London

Poems 1930–1989 first published in 2002 by
Calder Publications Ltd.,
London.

This volume contains all material previously published in *Poems in English*,
Poems in English and French, and *Poems 1930–1978*, with new
unpublished material from different sources.
The Early Poems at the end of the volume have appeared in
Samuel Beckett: Poet and Critic by Laurence Harvey. Some individual
poems published here in book form for the first time appeared in
periodicals during or after the author's lifetime.

French poems appear with the permission of Editions de
Minuit, Paris.

British Library Cataloguing in Publication Data

Beckett, Samuel
Poems 1930–1989
I. Title
ISBN 0–7145–4186–9 cased
ISBN 0–7145–4290–3 paper (2004 A.D.)

British library cataloguing data is available on application.

Typeset in India by Kolam, Pondicherry.
Printed and bound in Great Britain
by MPG Books Ltd, Bodmin, Cornwall, UK.

CONTENTS

VII

FOREWORD

This is the fourth edition of Samuel Beckett's poems to appear in Britain since the Second World War, and it is considerably larger than its predecessors. It begins, as with earlier editions, with *Whoroscope*, written in a single night in 1930 as is explained in the Notes, and it finishes with a final section of even earlier work, which can be classified as juvenilia and would be unsuitable to open the volume. These would probably be unknown to us but for their appearance in Laurence Harvey's book on Beckett (1970), now difficult to obtain, in which they first appeared (See Notes).

The largest number of additions are in the post-war sections, both those written in English and those in French. It was originally intended to print translations by other hands of all the French poems into English, but the controversy that must accompany such an initiative not only caused a delay in the publication of the present volume, but led to a decision that it would be wiser to only use work by Mr Beckett himself. The translations given here are all the author's own; otherwise the French poems are not translated. In cases where there is a similarity or a reworking of the same theme that constitutes a variant, but not a translation, the poems appear in their own language section.

The *Mirlitonnades* or 'bird calls' have been extended from the last collection and reveal the late Beckett, often filling in time on his own in cafés, and finding words for a random thought. Sometimes playful, often sombre, they catch, with a total economy of words, the same preoccupations and insights into the human condition that can be found in the novels and plays.

The section containing translations of other French poets has not been enlarged, with one exception, although there are other translations that have appeared in pre-war magazines. Mr Beckett considered these to have been hasty work done to earn a little money before such drudgery became unnecessary, and we have respected his wishes. His translations from Spanish, in the *Anthology of Mexican Poetry* edited by Vittorio Paz, are separately available.

From the beginning of his literary career Samuel Beckett was a true poet, and his lyrical gift and ear for cadence, melody and scansion is evident in all his work and was certainly present in the plays and novels, which are never far from poetry. His love of Dante and the German romantic poets often surfaces, as does his feeling for Shakespeare and the King James Bible, while the poets who were prominent in his youth, T.S. Eliot in particular, had an obvious influence on *Whoroscope* and the even earlier poems given at the end of this volume. The Joycean influence is more evident in the early prose than in the poetry.

There is great variety in the *Poems* 1930–1989, with time narrowing the style to simplicity and concision, but the poems always accurately reflect what he was writing in other forms at the same time, as well as what was relevant to his life. Poems that were obviously written at a period of occasional irritation must not be taken to convey a permanent attitude. False impressions have been given by some, especially composers who have set certain poems and have selected those which appeared to share their own attitudes. Beckett has always appealed to musicians and some poems have been set many times, but the difficulty composers have encountered has had much to do with the music that is already present in Beckett's cadences and makes enhancement almost impossible. It should also be said that apart from the pleasure and insight the poems offer to readers, they are also an excellent introduction to the work of a genius who many believe to be the major creative writer of the twentieth century.

The Publishers.

PART I

POEMS IN ENGLISH

1. WHOROSCOPE

Whoroscope

What's that?
An egg?
By the brothers Boot it stinks fresh.
Give it to Gillot.

Galileo how are you
and his consecutive thirds!
The vile old Copernican lead-swinging son of a sutler!
We're moving he said we're off— Porca Madonna!
the way a boatswain would be, or a sack-of-potatoey
                          charging Pretender.

That's not moving, that's *moving*.   10

What's that?
A little green fry or a mushroomy one?
Two lashed ovaries with prostisciutto?
How long did she womb it, the feathery one?
Three days and four nights?
Give it to Gillot.

Faulhaber, Beeckman and Peter the Red,
come now in the cloudy avalanche or Gassendi's sun-red
                              crystally cloud
and I'll pebble you all your hen-and-a-half ones
or I'll pebble a lens under the quilt in the midst of day.   20

To think he was my own brother, Peter the Bruiser,
and not a syllogism out of him
no more than if Pa were still in it.
Hey! pass over those coppers,
sweet millèd sweat of my burning liver!
Them were the days I sat in the hot-cupboard throwing
                                      Jesuits out of the skylight.

Who's that? Hals?
Let him wait.

My squinty doaty!
I hid and you sook.   30
And Francine my precious fruit of a house-and-parlour
                                                    foetus!
What an exfoliation!
Her little grey flayed epidermis and scarlet tonsils!
My one child
scourged by a fever to stagnant murky blood—
blood!
Oh Harvey belovèd
how shall the red and white, the many in the few,
(dear bloodswirling Harvey)
eddy through that cracked beater?   40
And the fourth Henry came to the crypt of the arrow.

What's that?
How long?
Sit on it.

4

A wind of evil flung my despair of ease
against the sharp spires of the one
lady:
not once or twice but...
(Kip of Christ hatch it!)
in one sun's drowning   50
(Jesuitasters please copy).
So on with the silk hose over the knitted, and the morbid
                                                        leather—
what am I saying! the gentle canvas—
and away to Ancona on the bright Adriatic,
and farewell for a space to the yellow key of the
                                                Rosicrucians.
They don't know what the master of them that do did,
that the nose is touched by the kiss of all foul and sweet air,
and the drums, and the throne of the faecal inlet,
and the eyes by its zig-zags.
So we drink Him and eat Him   60
and the watery Beaune and the stale cubes of Hovis
because He can jig
as near or as far from His Jigging Self
and as sad or lively as the chalice or the tray asks.
How's that, Antonio?

In the name of Bacon will you chicken me up that egg.
Shall I swallow cave-phantoms?

Anna Maria!
She reads Moses and says her love is crucified.
Leider! Leider! she bloomed and withered,   70
a pale abusive parakeet in a mainstreet window.

5

No I believe every word of it I assure you.
Fallor, ergo sum!
The coy old frôleur!
He tolle'd and legge'd
and he buttoned on his redemptorist waistcoat.
No matter, let it pass.
I'm a bold boy I know
so I'm not my son
(even if I were a concierge)   80
nor Joachim my father's
but the chip of a perfect block that's neither old nor new,
the lonely petal of a great high bright rose.

Are you ripe at last,
my slim pale double-breasted turd?
How rich she smells,
this abortion of a fledgling!
I will eat it with a fish fork.
White and yolk and feathers.
Then I will rise and move moving   90
toward Rahab of the snows,
the murdering matinal pope-confessed amazon,
Christina the ripper.
Oh Weulles spare the blood of a Frank
who has climbed the bitter steps,
(René du Perron... !)
and grant me my second
starless inscrutable hour.

1930

NOTES *(by the author)*

René Descartes, Seigneur du Perron, liked his omelette made of eggs hatched from eight to ten days; shorter or longer under the hen and the result, he says, is disgusting.

He kept his own birthday to himself so that no astrologer could cast his nativity.

The shuttle of a ripening egg combs the warp of his days.

P. 3, 1.	3	In 1640 the brothers Boot refuted Aristotle in Dublin.
	4	Descartes passed on the easier problems in analytical geometry to his valet Gillot.
	5–10	Refer to his comtempt for Galileo Jr., (whom he confused with the more musical Galileo Sr.), and to his expedient sophistry concerning the movement of the earth.
	17	He solved problems submitted by these mathematicians.
P. 4, 1.	21–26	The attempt at swindling on the part of his elder brother Pierre de la Bretaillière—The money he received as a soldier.
	27	Franz Hals.
	29–30	As a child he played with a little cross-eyed girl.
	31–35	His daughter died of scarlet fever at the age of six.
	37–40	Honoured Harvey for his discovery of the circulation of the blood, but would not admit that he had explained the motion of the heart.
	41	The heart of Henri IV was received at the Jesuit college of La Flèche while Descartes was still a student there.
P. 5, 1.	45–53	His visions and pilgrimage to Loretto.
	56–65	His Eucharistic sophistry, in reply to the Jansenist Antoine Arnauld, who challenged him to reconcile his doctrine of matter with the doctrine of transubstantiation.

2. GNOME

Gnome

Spend the years of learning squandering
Courage for the years of wandering
Through a world politely turning
From the loutishness of learning

1934

3. HOME OLGA

Home Olga

J might be made sit up for a jade of hope (and exile,
                                        don't you know)
And Jesus and Jesuits juggernauted in the haemorrhoidal isle,
Modo et forma anal maiden, giggling to death in stomacho.
E for the erythrite of love and silence and the sweet noo
                                        style,
Swoops and loops of love and silence in the eye of the sun
                                        and view of the mew,
Juvante Jah and a Jain or two and the tip of a friendly
                                        yiddophile.
O for an opal of faith and cunning winking adieu, adieu,
                                        adieu.
Yesterday shall be tomorrow, riddle me that my rapparee.
Che sarà sarà che fu, there's more than Homer knows how
                                        to spew,
Exempli gratia: ecce himself and the pickthank agnus
                                        —e.o.o.e.

1932

4. ECHO'S BONES

The Vulture

dragging his hunger through the sky
of my skull shell of sky and earth

stooping to the prone who must
soon take up their life and walk

mocked by a tissue that may not serve
till hunger earth and sky be offal

Enueg I

Exeo in a spasm
tired of my darling's red sputum
from the Portobello Private Nursing Home
its secret things
and toil to the crest of the surge of the steep perilous bridge
and lapse down blankly under the scream of the hoarding
round the bright stiff banner of the hoarding
into a black west
throttled with clouds.

Above the mansions the algum-trees
the mountains
my skull sullenly
clot of anger
skewered aloft strangled in the cang of the wind
bites like a dog against its chastisement.

I trundle along rapidly now on my ruined feet
flush with the livid canal;
at Parnell Bridge a dying barge
carrying a cargo of nails and timber
rocks itself softly in the foaming cloister of the lock;
on the far bank a gang of down and outs would seem to
be mending a beam.

Then for miles only wind
and the weals creeping alongside on the water
and the world opening up to the south
across a travesty of champaign to the mountains
and the stillborn evening turning a filthy green
manuring the night fungus
and the mind annulled
wrecked in wind.

I splashed past a little wearish old man,
Democritus,
scuttling along between a crutch and a stick,
his stump caught up horribly, like a claw, under his

                                 breech,
smoking.
Then because a field on the left went up in a sudden blaze
of shouting and urgent whistling and scarlet and blue

                                 ganzies
I stopped and climbed the bank to see the game.
A child fidgeting at the gate called up:
"Would we be let in Mister?"
"Certainly" I said "you would."
But, afraid, he set off down the road.
"Well" I called after him "why wouldn't you go on in?"
"Oh" he said, knowingly,
"I was in that field before and I got put out."
So on,
derelict,
as from a bush of gorse on fire in the mountain after dark,
or in Sumatra the jungle hymen,
the still flagrant rafflesia.

Next:
a lamentable family of grey verminous hens,
perishing out in the sunk field,
trembling, half asleep, against the closed door of a shed,
with no means of roosting.

The great mushy toadstool,
green-black,
oozing up after me,
soaking up the tattered sky like an ink of pestilence,
in my skull the wind going fetid,
the water...

Next:
on the hill down from the Fox and Geese into Chapelizod
a small malevolent goat, exiled on the road,
remotely pucking the gate of his field;
the Isolde Stores a great perturbation of sweaty heroes,
in their Sunday best,
come hastening down for a pint of nepenthe or moly or
                                        half and half
from watching the hurlers above in Kilmainham.

Blotches of doomed yellow in the pit of the Liffey;
the fingers of the ladders hooked over the parapet,
soliciting;
a slush of vigilant gulls in the grey spew of the sewer.

Ah the banner
the banner of meat bleeding
on the silk of the seas and the arctic flowers
that do not exist.

14

Enueg II

world world world world
and the face grave
cloud against the evening

de morituris nihil nisi

and the face crumbling shyly
too late to darken the sky
blushing away into the evening
shuddering away like a gaffe

veronica mundi
veronica munda
give us a wipe for the love of Jesus

sweating like Judas
tired of dying
tired of policemen
feet in marmalade
perspiring profusely
heart in marmalade
smoke more fruit
the old heart the old heart
breaking outside congress
doch I assure thee
lying on O'Connell Bridge

goggling at the tulips of the evening
the green tulips
shining round the corner like an anthrax
shining on Guinness's barges

the overtone the face
too late to brighten the sky
doch doch I assure thee

Alba

before morning you shall be here
and Dante and the Logos and all strata and mysteries
and the branded moon
beyond the white plane of music
that you shall establish here before morning

      grave suave singing silk
      stoop to the black firmament of areca
      rain on the bamboos flower of smoke alley of willows

who though you stoop with fingers of compassion
to endorse the dust
shall not add to your bounty
whose beauty shall be a sheet before me
a statement of itself drawn across the tempest of emblems
so that there is no sun and no unveiling
and no host
only I and then the sheet
and bulk dead

Dortmunder

In the magic the Homer dusk
past the red spire of sanctuary
I null she royal hulk
hasten to the violet lamp to the thin K'in music of the bawd.
She stands before me in the bright stall
sustaining the jade splinters
the scarred signaculum of purity quiet
the eyes the eyes black till the plagal east
shall resolve the long night phrase.
Then, as a scroll, folded,
and the glory of her dissolution enlarged
in me, Habbakuk, mard of all sinners.
Schopenhauer is dead, the bawd
puts her lute away.

Sanies I

all the livelong way this day of sweet showers from
                                        Portrane on the seashore
Donabate sad swans of Turvey Swords
pounding along in three ratios like a sonata
like a Ritter with pommelled scrotum atra cura on the step
Botticelli from the fork down pestling the transmission
tires bleeding voiding zeep the highway
all heaven in the sphincter
the sphincter

müüüüüüüüde now
potwalloping now through the promenaders
this trusty all-steel this super-real
bound for home like a good boy
where I was born with a pop with the green of the larches
ah to be back in the caul now with no trusts
no fingers no spoilt love
belting along in the meantime clutching the bike
the billows of the nubile the cere wrack
pot-valiant caulless waisted in rags hatless
for mamma papa chicken and ham
warm Grave too say the word
happy days snap the stem shed a tear
this day Spy Wedsday seven pentades past
oh the larches the pain drawn like a cork
the glans he took the day off up hill and down dale
with a ponderous fawn from the Liverpool London and
                                        Globe
back the shadows lengthen the sycomores are sobbing
to roly-poly oh to me a spanking boy

buckets of fizz childbed is thirsty work
for the midwife he is gory
for the proud parent he washes down a gob of gladness
for footsore Achates also he pants his pleasure
sparkling beestings for me
tired now hair ebbing gums ebbing ebbing home
good as gold now in the prime after a brief prodigality
yea and suave
suave urbane beyond good and evil
biding my time without rancour you may take your oath
distraught half-crooked courting the sneers of these fauns
                                        these smart nymphs
clipped like a pederast as to one trouser-end
sucking in my bloated lantern behind a Wild Woodbine
cinched to death in a filthy slicker
flinging the proud Swift forward breasting the swell of
                                        Stürmers
I see main verb at last
her whom alone in the accusative
I have dismounted to love
gliding towards me dauntless nautch-girl on the face of the
                                        waters
dauntless daughter of desires in the old black and flamingo
get along with you now take the six the seven the eight or
                                the little single-decker
take a bus for all I care walk cadge a lift
home to the cob of your web in Holles Street
and let the tiger go on smiling
in our hearts that funds ways home

Sanies II

there was a happy land
the American Bar
in Rue Mouffetard
there were red eggs there
I have a dirty I say henorrhoids
coming from the bath
the steam the delight the sherbet
the chagrin of the old skinnymalinks
slouching happy body
loose in my stinking old suit
sailing slouching up to Puvis the gauntlet of tulips
lash lash me with yaller tulips I will let down
my stinking old trousers
my love she sewed up the pockets alive the live-oh she did
       she said that was better
spotless then within the brown rags gliding
frescoward free up the fjord of dyed eggs and thongbells
I disappear don't you know into the local
the mackerel are at billiards there they are crying the scores
the Barfrau makes a big impression with her mighty bottom
Dante and blissful Beatrice are there
prior to Vita Nuova
the balls splash no luck comrade
Gracieuse is there Belle-Belle down the drain
booted Percinet with his cobalt jowl
they are necking gobble-gobble
suck is not suck that alters

lo Alighieri has got off au revoir to all that
I break down quite in a titter of despite
hark
upon the saloon a terrible hush
a shiver convulses Madame de la Motte
it courses it peals down her collops
the great bottom foams into stillness
quick quick the cavaletto supplejacks for mumbo-jumbo
vivas puellas mortui incurrrrrsant boves
oh subito subito ere she recover the cang bamboo for
                                                    bastinado
a bitter moon fessade à la mode
oh Becky spare me I have done thee no wrong spare me
                                                    damn thee
spare me good Becky
call off thine adders Becky I will compensate thee in full
Lord have mercy upon
Christ have mercy upon us

Lord have mercy upon us

Serena I

without the grand old British Museum
Thales and the Aretino
on the bosom of the Regent's Park the phlox
crackles under the thunder
scarlet beauty in our world dead fish adrift
all things full of gods
pressed down and bleeding
a weaver-bird is tangerine the harpy is past caring
the condor likewise in his mangy boa
they stare out across monkey-hill the elephants
Ireland
the light creeps down their old home canyon
sucks me aloof to that old reliable
the burning btm of George the drill
ah across the way a adder
broaches her rat
white as snow
in her dazzling oven strom of peristalsis
limae labor

ah father father that art in heaven

I find me taking the Crystal Palace
for the Blessed Isles from Primrose Hill
alas I must be that kind of person
hence in Ken Wood who shall find me

my breath held in the midst of thickets
none but the most quarried lovers

I surprise me moved by the many a funnel hinged
for the obeisance to Tower Bridge
the viper's curtsy to and from the City
till in the dusk a lighter
blind with pride
tosses aside the scarf of the bascules
then in the grey hold of the ambulance
throbbing on the brink ebb of sighs
then I hug me below among the canaille
until a guttersnipe blast his cernèd eyes
demanding 'ave I done with the Mirror
I stump off in a fearful rage under Married Men's Quarters
Bloody Tower
and afar off at all speed screw me up Wren's giant bully
and curse the day caged panting on the platform
under the flaring urn
I was not born Defoe

but in Ken Wood
who shall find me

my brother the fly
the common housefly
sidling out of darkness into light
fastens on his place in the sun
whets his six legs
revels in his planes his poisers
it is the autumn of his life
he could not serve typhoid and mammon

Serena II

this clonic earth

see-saw she is blurred in sleep
she is fat half dead the rest is free-wheeling
part the black shag the pelt
is ashen woad
snarl and howl in the wood wake all the birds
hound the harlots out of the ferns
this damfool twilight threshing in the brake
bleating to be bloodied
this crapulent hush
tear its heart out

in her dreams she trembles again
way back in the dark old days panting
in the claws of the Pins in the stress of her hour
the bag writhes she thinks she is dying
the light fails it is time to lie down
Clew Bay vat of xanthic flowers
Croagh Patrick waned Hindu to spite a pilgrim
she is ready she has lain down above all the islands of glory
straining now this Sabbath evening of garlands
with a yo-heave-ho of able-bodied swans
out from the doomed land their reefs of tresses
in a hag she drops her young
the whales in Blacksod Bay are dancing

the asphodels come running the flags after
she thinks she is dying she is ashamed

she took me up on to a watershed
whence like the rubrics of a childhood
behold Meath shining through a chink in the hills
posses of larches there is no going back on
a rout of tracks and streams fleeing to the sea
kindergartens of steeples and then the harbour
like a woman making to cover her breasts
and left me

with whatever trust of panic we went out
with so much shall we return
there shall be no loss of panic between a man and his dog
bitch though he be

sodden packet of Churchman
muzzling the cairn
it is worse than dream
the light randy slut can't be easy
this clonic earth
all these phantoms shuddering out of focus
it is useless to close the eyes
all the chords of the earth broken like a woman pianist's
the toads abroad again on their rounds
sidling up to their snares
the fairy-tales of Meath ended
so say your prayers now and go to bed
your prayers before the lamps start to sing behind the larches
here at these knees of stone
then to bye-bye on the bones

26

Serena III

fix this pothook of beauty on this palette
you never know it might be final

or leave her she is paradise and then
plush hymens on your eyeballs

or on Butt Bridge blush for shame
the mixed declension of those mammae
cock up thy moon thine and thine only
up up up to the star of evening
swoon upon the arch-gasometer
on Misery Hill brand-new carnation
swoon upon the little purple
house of prayer
something heart of Mary
the Bull and Pool Beg that will never meet
not in this world

whereas dart away through the cavorting scapes
bucket o'er Victoria Bridge that's the idea
slow down slink down the Ringsend Road
Irishtown Sandymount puzzle find the Hell Fire
the Merrion Flats scored with a thrillion sigmas
Jesus Christ Son of God Saviour His Finger
girls taken strippin that's the idea
on the Bootersgrad breakwind and water
the tide making the dun gulls in a panic
the sands quicken in your hot heart
hide yourself not in the Rock keep on the move
keep on the move

Malacoda

thrice he came
the undertaker's man
impassible behind his scutal bowler

to measure
is he not paid to measure
this incorruptible in the vestibule
this malebranca knee-deep in the lilies
Malacoda knee-deep in the lilies
Malacoda for all the expert awe
that felts his perineum mutes his signal
sighing up through the heavy air
must it be it must be it must be
find the weeds engage them in the garden
hear she may see she need not

to coffin
with assistant ungulata
find the weeds engage their attention
hear she must see she need not

to cover
to be sure cover cover all over
your targe allow me hold your sulphur
divine dogday glass set fair
stay Scarmilion stay stay
lay this Huysum on the box
mind the imago it is he
hear she must see she must
all aboard all souls
half-mast aye aye

nay

Da Tagte Es

redeem the surrogate goodbyes
the sheet astream in your hand
who have no more for the land
and the glass unmisted above your eyes

Echo's Bones

asylum under my tread all this day
their muffled revels as the flesh falls
breaking without fear or favour wind
the gantelope of sense and nonsense run
taken by the maggots for what they are

1935

5. EIGHT POEMS

Cascando

I

why not merely the despaired of
occasion of
wordshed

is it not better abort than be barren

the hours after you are gone are so leaden
they will always start dragging too soon
the grapples clawing blindly the bed of want
bringing up the bones the old loves
sockets filled once with eyes like yours
all always is it better too soon than never
the black want splashing their faces
saying again nine days never floated the loved
nor nine months
nor nine lives

2
saying again
if you do not teach me I shall not learn
saying again there is a last
even of last times
last times of begging
last times of loving
of knowing not knowing pretending
a last even of last times of saying
if you do not love me I shall not be loved
if I do not love you I shall not love

the churn of stale words in the heart again
love love love thud of the old plunger
pestling the unalterable
whey of words

terrified again
of not loving
of loving and not you
of being loved and not by you
of knowing not knowing pretending
pretending

I and all the others that will love you
if they love you

3
unless they love you

1936

Ooftish

offer it up plank it down
Golgotha was only the potegg
cancer angina it is all one to us
cough up your T.B. don't be stingy
no trifle is too trifling not even a thrombus
anything venereal is especially welcome
that old toga in the mothballs
don't be sentimental you won't be wanting it again
send it along we'll put it in the pot with the rest
with your love requited and unrequited
the things taken too late the things taken too soon
the spirit aching bullock's scrotum
you won't cure it you won't endure it
it is you it equals you any fool has to pity you
so parcel up the whole issue and send it along
the whole misery diagnosed undiagnosed misdiagnosed
get your friends to do the same we'll make use of it
we'll make sense of it we'll put it in the pot with the rest
it all boils down to blood of lamb

1938

Saint-Lô

Vire will wind in other shadows
unborn through the bright ways tremble
and the old mind ghost-forsaken
sink into its havoc

1946

34

dread nay

head fast
in out as dead
till rending
long still
faint stir
unseal the eye
till still again
seal again

head sphere
ashen smooth
one eye
no hint when to
then glare
cyclop no
one side
eerily

on face
of out spread
vast in
the highmost
snow white
sheeting all
asylum head
sole blot

faster than where
in hellice eyes
stream till
frozen to
jaws rail
gnaw gnash
teeth with stork
clack chatter

come through
no sense and gone
while eye
shocked wide
with white
still to bare
stir dread
nay to nought

sudden in
ashen smooth
aghast
glittering rent
till sudden
smooth again
stir so past
never been

at ray
in latibule
long dark
stir of dread
till breach
long sealed
dark again
still again

so ere
long still
long nought
rent so
so stir
long past
head fast
in out as dead

1974

Something there

something there
where
out there
out where
outside
what
the head what else
something there somewhere outside
the head

at the faint sound so brief
it is gone and the whole globe
not yet bare
the eye
opens wide
wide
till in the end
nothing more
shutters it again

so the odd time
out there
somewhere out there
like as if
as if
something
not life
necessarily

1974

Roundelay

on all that strand
at end of day
steps sole sound
long sole sound
until unbidden stay
then no sound
on all that strand
long no sound
until unbidden go
steps sole sound
long sole sound
on all that strand
at end of day

1976

thither

thither
a far cry
for one
so little
fair daffodils
march then

then there
then there

then thence
daffodils
again
march then
again
a far cry
again
for one
so little

1976

SONG

Age is when to a man
Huddled o'er the ingle
Shivering for the hag
To put the pan in the bed
And bring the toddy
She comes in the ashes
Who loved could not be won
Or won not loved
Or some other trouble
Comes in the ashes
Like in that old light
The face in the ashes
That old starlight
On the earth again.

1962

6. TWO PREVIOUSLY UNPUBLISHED POEMS

Antipepsis

And the number was uneven
In the green of holy Stephen
Where before the ass the cart
Was harnessed for a foreign part.
In this should not be seen the sign
Of hasard, no, but of design,
For of the two, by common consent,
The cart was the more intelligent.
Whose exceptionally pia
Mater hatched this grand idea
Is not known. He or she,
Smiling, unmolested, free,
By this one act the mind become
A providential vacuum,
Continues still to stroll amok,
To eat, drink, piss, shit, fart and fuck,
Assuming that the fucking season
Did not expire with that of reason.
Now through the city spreads apace
The cry: A thought has taken place!
A human thought! Ochone! Ochone!
Purissima Virgo! We're undone!
Bitched, buggered and bewilderèd!
Bring forth your dead! Bring forth your dead!

The Downs

the downs
summer days on the downs
hand in hand
one loving
one loved
back at night
the hut

no thought
thoughtless on
under the sun
hand in hand
one loving
the other loved
thoughtless back
night

on till the cliff
the edge
hand in hand
gazing down
the foam
no further
the edge
the foam

no speech
speechless on
under the sun
hand in hand
till the edge
speechless back
the hut
night

the bridge
winter night
wind
snow
gazing down
the flood
foaming on
black flood foaming on

no thought
gazing down
meaningless flood
foaming on
winter night
wind
snow
no meaning

light
from the banks
lamplight
to light the foam
the snow
faintly lit
the foam
the snow

7. LATE POEMS

one dead of night
in the dead still
he looked up
from his book

from that dark
to pore on other dark

till afar
taper faint
the eyes

in the dead still

till afar
his book as by
a hand not his
a hand on his
faintly closed

for good or ill

for good and ill

Stuttgart
26.6.77

Cimetière St. André*
Caroline Hay Taylor
morte en Irlande august 32

One who never turned her back but
    marched breast forward
never doubted clouds would break
never dreamed though right were
    worsted wrong would triumph
held we fall to rise, are baffled to fight better, sleep to wake

* See also page 90 for another version

Go where never before
No sooner there than there always
No matter where never before
No sooner there than there always

Brief Dream

go end there
one fine day
where never till then
till as much as to say
no matter where
no matter when

PART II

POEMS IN FRENCH
with some translations by the author

1. POÈMES 1937–1939

elles viennent
autres et pareilles
avec chacune c'est autre et c'est pareil
avec chacune l'absence d'amour est autre
avec chacune l'absence d'amour est pareille

they come
different and the same
with each it is different and the same
with each the absence of love is different
with each the absence of love is the same

à elle l'acte calme
les pores savants le sexe bon enfant
l'attente pas trop lente les regrets pas trop longs l'absence
au service de la présence
les quelques haillons d'azur dans la tête les points enfin
                                        morts du coeur
toute la tardive grâce d'une pluie cessant
au tomber d'une nuit
d'août

à elle vide
lui pur
d'amour

être là sans mâchoires sans dents
où s'en va le plaisir de perdre
avec celui à peine inférieur
de gagner
et Roscelin et on attend
adverbe oh petit cadeau
vide vide sinon des loques de chanson
mon père m'a donné un mari
ou en faisant la fleur
qu'elle mouille
tant qu'elle voudra jusqu'à l'élégie
des sabots ferrés encore loin des Halles
ou l'eau de la canaille pestant dans les tuyaux
ou plus rien
qu'elle mouille puisque c'est ainsi
parfasse tout le superflu
et vienne
à la bouche idiote à la main formicante
au bloc cave à l'oeil qui écoute
de lointains coups de ciseaux argentins

Ascension

à travers la mince cloison
ce jour où un enfant
prodigue à sa façon
rentra dans sa famille
j'entends la voix
elle est émue elle commente
la coupe du monde de football

toujours trop jeune

en même temps par la fenêtre ouverte
par les airs tout court
sourdement
la houle des fidèles

son sang gicla avec abondance
sur les draps sur les pois de senteur sur son mec
de ses doigts dégoûtants il ferma les paupières
sur les grands yeux verts étonnés

elle rôde légère
sur ma tombe d'air

La Mouche

entre la scène et moi
la vitre
vide sauf elle

ventre à terre
sanglée dans ses boyaux noirs
antennes affolées ailes liées
pattes crochues bouche suçant à vide
sabrant l'azur s'écrasant contre l'invisible
sous mon pouce impuissant elle fait chavirer
la mer et le ciel serein

musique de l'indifférence
coeur temps air feu sable
du silence éboulement d'amours
couvre leurs voix et que
je ne m'entende plus
me taire

bois seul
bouffe brûle fornique crève seul comme devant
les absents sont morts les présents puent
sors tes yeux détourne-les sur les roseaux
se taquinent-ils ou les aïs
pas la peine il y a le vent
et l'état de veille

ainsi a-t-on beau
par le beau temps et par le mauvais
enfermé chez soi enfermé chez eux
comme si c'était d'hier se rappeler le mammouth
le dinothérium les premiers baisers
les périodes glaciaires n'apportant rien de neuf
la grande chaleur du treizième de leur ère
sur Lisbonne fumante Kant froidement penché
rêver en générations de chênes et oublier son père
ses yeux s'il portait la moustache
s'il était bon de quoi il est mort
on n'en est pas moins mangé sans appétit
par le mauvais temps et par le pire
enfermé chez soi enfermé chez eux

Rue de Vaugirard

à mi-hauteur
je débraye et béant de candeur
expose la plaque aux lumières et aux ombres
puis repars fortifié
d'un négatif irrécusable

Dieppe

encore le dernier reflux
le galet mort
le demi-tour puis les pas
vers les vieilles lumières

Dieppe

again the last ebb
the dead shingle
the turning then the steps
towards the lights of old

Arènes de Lutèce

De là où nous sommes assis plus haut que les gradins
je nous vois entrer du côté de la Rue des Arènes,
hésiter, regarder en l'air, puis pesamment
venir vers nous à travers le sable sombre,
de plus en plus laids, aussi laids que les autres,
mais muets. Un petit chien vert
entre en courant du côté de la Rue Monge,
elle s'arrête, elle le suit des yeux,
il traverse l'arène, il disparait
derrière le socle du savant Gabriel de Mortillet.
Elle se retourne, je suis parti, je gravis seul
les marches rustiques, je touche de ma main gauche
la rampe rustique, elle est en béton. Elle hésite,
fait un pas vers la sortie de la Rue Monge, puis me suit.
J'ai un frisson, c'est moi qui me rejoins,
c'est avec d'autres yeux que maintenant je regarde
le sable, les flaques d'eau sous la bruine,
une petite fille traînant derrière elle un cerceau,
un couple, qui sait des amoureux, la main dans la main,
les gradins vides, les hautes maisons, le ciel
qui nous éclaire trop tard.
Je me retourne, je suis étonné
de trouver là son triste visage.

jusque dans la caverne ciel et sol
et une à une les vieilles voix
d'outre-tombe
et lentement la même lumière
qui sur les plaines d'Enna en longs viols
macérait naguère les capillaires
et les mêmes lois
que naguère
et lentement au loin qui éteint
Proserpine et Atropos
adorable de vide douteux
encore la bouche d'ombre

2. *Six Poèmes* 1947–1949

bon bon il est un pays
où l'oubli où pèse l'oubli
doucement sur les mondes innommés
là la tête on la tait la tête est muette
et on sait non on ne sait rien
le chant des bouches mortes meurt
sur la grève il a fait le voyage
il n'y a rien à pleurer

ma solitude je la connais allez je la connais mal
j'ai le temps c'est ce que je me dis j'ai le temps
mais quel temps os affamé le temps du chien
du ciel pâlissant sans cesse mon grain de ciel
du rayon qui grimpe ocellé tremblant
des microns des années ténèbres

vous voulez que j'aille d'A à B je ne peux pas
je ne peux pas sortir je suis dans un pays sans traces
oui oui c'est une belle chose que vous avez là une bien
                                                    belle chose
qu'est-ce que c'est ne me posez plus de questions
spirale poussière d'instants qu'est-ce que c'est le même
le calme l'amour la haine le calme le calme

Mort de A.D.

et là être là encore là
pressé contre ma vieille planche vérolée du noir
des jours et nuits broyés aveuglément
à être là à ne pas fuir et fuir et être là
courbé vers l'aveu du temps mourant
d'avoir été ce qu'il fut fait ce qu'il fit
de moi de mon ami mort hier l'oeil luisant
les dents longues haletant dans sa barbe dévorant
la vie des saints une vie par jour de vie
revivant dans la nuit ses noirs péchés
mort hier pendant que je vivais
et être là buvant plus haut que l'orage
la coulpe du temps irrémissible
agrippé au vieux bois témoin des départs
témoin des retours

vive morte ma seule saison
lis blancs chrysanthèmes
nids vifs abandonnés
boue des feuilles d'avril
beaux jours gris de givre

je suis ce cours de sable qui glisse
entre le galet et la dune
la pluie d'été pleut sur ma vie
sur moi ma vie qui me fuit me poursuit
et finira le jour de son commencement

cher instant je te vois
dans ce rideau de brume qui recule
où je n'aurai plus à fouler ces longs seuils mouvants
et vivrai le temps d'une porte
qui s'ouvre et se referme

my way is in the sand flowing
between the shingle and the dune
the summer rain rains on my life
on me my life harrying fleeing
to its beginning to its end

my peace is there in the receding mist
when I may cease from treading these long shifting
                                        thresholds
and live the space of a door
that opens and shuts

que ferais-je sans ce monde sans visage sans questions
où être ne dure qu'un instant où chaque instant
verse dans le vide dans l'oubli d'avoir été
sans cette onde où à la fin
corps et ombre ensemble s'engloutissent
que ferais-je sans ce silence gouffre des murmures
haletant furieux vers le secours vers l'amour
sans ce ciel qui s'élève
sur la poussière de ses lests

que ferais-je je ferais comme hier comme aujourd'hui
regardant par mon hublot si je ne suis pas seul
à errer et à virer loin de toute vie
dans un espace pantin
sans voix parmi les voix
enfermées avec moi

what would I do without this world faceless incurious
where to be lasts but an instant where every instant
spills in the void the ignorance of having been
without this wave where in the end
body and shadow together are engulfed
what would I do without this silence where the murmurs die
the pantings the frenzies towards succour towards love
without this sky that soars
above its ballast dust

what would I do what I did yesterday and the day before
peering out of my deadlight looking for another
wandering like me eddying far from all the living
in a convulsive space
among the voices voiceless
that throng my hiddenness

je voudrais que mon amour meure
qu'il pleuve sur le cimetière
et les ruelles où je vais
pleurant celle qui crut m'aimer

I would like my love to die
and the rain to be raining on the graveyard
and on me walking the streets
mourning her who thought she loved me

3. Poème

hors crâne seul dedans
quelque part quelquefois
comme quelque chose

crâne abri dernier
pris dans le dehors
tel Bocca dans la glace

l'oeil à l'alarme infime
s'ouvre bée se rescelle
n'y ayant plus rien

ainsi quelquefois
comme quelque chose
de la vie pas forcément
1974

4. *Mirlitonnades*

en face
le pire
jusqu'à ce
qu'il fasse rire

rentrer
à la nuit
au logis
allumer

éteindre voir
la nuit voir
collé à la vitre
le visage

somme toute
tout compte fait
un quart de milliasse
de quarts d'heure
sans compter
les temps morts

fin fond du néant
au bout de quelle guette
l'oeil crut entrevoir
remuer faiblement
la tête le calma disant
ce ne fut que dans ta tête

silence tel que ce qui fut
avant jamais ne sera plus
par le murmure déchiré
d'une parole sans passé
d'avoir trop dit n'en pouvant plus
jurant de ne se taire plus

écoute-les
s'ajouter
les mots
aux mots
sans mot
les pas
aux pas
un à
un

lueurs lisières
de la navette
plus qu'un pas s'éteignent
demi-tour remiroitent

halte plutôt
loin des deux
chez soi sans soi
ni eux

imagine si ceci
un jour ceci
un beau jour
imagine
si un jour
un beau jour ceci
cessait
imagine

d'abord
à plat sur du dur
la droite
ou la gauche
n'importe

ensuite
à plat sur la droite
ou la gauche
la gauche
ou la droite

enfin
à plat sur la gauche
ou la droite
n'importe
sur le tout
la tête

flux cause
que toute chose
tout en étant
toute chose
donc celle-là
même celle-là
tout en étant
n'est pas
parlons-en

samedi répit
plus rire
depuis minuit
jusqu'à minuit
plus pleurer

*

chaque jour envie
d'être un jour en vie
non certes sans regret
un jour d'être né

nuit qui fais tant
implorer l'aube
nuit de grâce
tombe

*

rien nul
n'aura été
pour rien
tant été
rien
nul

à peine à bien mené
le dernier pas le pied
repose en attendant
comme le veut l'usage
que l'autre en fasse autant
comme le veut l'usage
et porte ainsi le faix
encore de l'avant
comme le veut l'usage
enfin jusqu'à présent

ce qu'ont les yeux
mal vu de bien
les doigts lassés
de bien filer
serre-les bien
les doigts les yeux
le bien revient
en mieux

ce qu'a de pis
le coeur connu
la tête pu
de pis se dire
fais-les
ressusciter
le pis revient
en pire

ne manquez pas à Tanger
le cimetière Saint-André
morts sous un fouillis
de fleurs surensevelis
banc à la mémoire
d'Arthur Keyser
de coeur avec lui
restes dessus assis

plus loin un autre commémore
Caroline Hay Taylor
fidèle à sa philosophie
qu'espoir il y a tant qu'il y a vie
d'Irlande elle s'enfuit aux cieux
en août mil neuf cent trente-deux

ne manquez pas à Stuttgart
la longue Rue Neckar
du néant là l'attrait
n'est plus ce qu'il était
tant le soupçon est fort
d'y être déjà et d'ores

vieil aller
vieux arrêts

aller
absent
absent
arrêter

fous qui disiez
plus jamais
vite
redites

pas à pas
nulle part
nul seul
ne sait comment
petits pas
nulle part
obstinément

rêve
sans fin
ni trêve
à rien

morte parmi
ses mouches mortes
un souffle coulis
berce l'araignée

*

d'où
la voix qui dit
vis

d'une autre vie

mots survivants
de la vie
encore un moment
tenez-lui compagnie

*

fleuves et océans
l'ont laissé pour vivant
au ru de Courtablon
près la Mare-Chaudron

de pied ferme
tout en n'attendant plus
il se passe devant
allant sans but

sitôt sorti de l'ermitage
ce fut le calme après l'orage

à l'instant de s'entendre dire
ne plus en avoir pour longtemps
la vie à lui enfin sourire
se mit de toutes ses dents

la nuit venue où l'âme allait
enfin lui être réclamée
voilà-t-il pas qu'incontinent
il la rendit une heure avant

pas davantage
de souvenirs qu'à l'âge
d'avril un jour
d'un jour

son ombre une nuit
lui reparut
s'allongea pâlit
se dissolut

noire sœur
qui es aux enfers
à tort tranchant
et à travers
qu'est-ce que tu attends

comme au
berceau
toute parole mue
comme au
berceau
folie à nouveau mine

*

c'est l'heure
du voir
le coeur
parti

à bout de songes un bouquin
au gîte à dire adieu astreint
de chasse lasse fit exprès
d'oublier le chandelier

le nain nonagénaire
dans un dernier murmure
de grâce au moins une bière
grandeur nature

ne verra t'il jamais
finir la nuit
où l'âme lui
sera réclamée

qu'à lever la tête
c'est la beauté
qu'à la lever
qu'à la
lever

par une faille dans l'inexistence
s'infiltrent des miasmes d'oxygène
dans le silence du pseudo-silence
dans la pénombre pur bonheur à peine

lui
à son âge
lui faire ça à lui
sacré canal
lacrymal

5. Comment dire

folie –
folie que de –
que de –
comment dire –
folie que de ce –
depuis –
folie depuis ce –
donné –
folie donné ce que de –
vu –
folie vu ce –
ce –
comment dire –
ceci –
ce ceci –
ceci-ci –
tout ce ceci-ci –
folie donné tout ce –
vu –
folie vu tout ce ceci-ci que de –
que de –
comment dire –
voir –
entrevoir –
croire entrevoir –
vouloir croire entrevoir –
folie que de vouloir croire entrevoir quoi –
quoi –
comment dire –
et où –

what is the word

folly –
folly for to –
for to –
what is the word –
folly from this –
all this –
folly from all this –
given –
folly given all this –
seeing –
folly seeing all this –
this –
what is the word –
this this –
this this here –
all this this here –
folly given all this –
seeing –
folly seeing all this this here –
for to –
what is the word –
see –
glimpse –
seem to glimpse –
need to seem to glimpse –
folly for to need to seem to glimpse –
what –
what is the word –
and where –

que de vouloir croire entrevoir quoi où –
où –
comment dire –
là –
là-bas –
loin –
loin là là-bas –
à peine –
loin là là-bas à peine quoi –
quoi –
comment dire –
vu tout ceci –
tout ce ceci-ci –
folie que de voir quoi –
entrevoir –
croire entrevoir –
vouloir croire entrevoir –
loin là là-bas à peine quoi –
folie que d'y vouloir croire entrevoir quoi –
quoi –
comment dire –

comment dire

29.10.88

folly for to need to seem to glimpse what where –
where –
what is the word –
there –
over there –
away over there –
afar –
afar away over there –
afaint –
afaint afar away over there what –
what –
what is the word –
seeing all this –
all this this –
all this this here –
folly for to see what –
glimpse –
seem to glimpse –
need to seem to glimpse –
afaint afar away over there what –
folly for to need to seem to glimpse afaint afar away over there
what –

what –
what is the word –

what is the word

PART III

TRANSLATIONS FROM FRENCH POETS
with the original poems

1. ALAIN BOSQUET

'Achetez mes soupirs'

Achetez mes soupirs.
Prenez mes doutes.
Je vous donne un cornet de grimaces?
Quand j'aurai tout vendu,
j'irai renaître loin de moi,
entre une mangue fraîche,
un baiser très félin,
quelques objects sans nom.
Achetez mes espoirs.
Prenez mes certitudes.
Je vous donne un cornet de sourirs?
Je suis le marchand des quatre raisons.

Fresh sighs for sale

Fresh sighs for sale!
Prime doubts a penny!
Scowls going at a loss!
When I'm sold out I'll go
far from me and these among
be born again:
a mango warm from the bough,
a more than feline kiss,
a few objects without name.
Fresh hopes for sale!
Prime sooth a penny!
Smiles going at a loss!
Bargains, bargains, in and out of reason!

2. PAUL ELUARD

L'amoureuse

Elle est debout sur mes paupières
Et ses cheveux sont dans les miens,
Elle a la forme de mes mains,
Elle a la couleur de mes yeux,
Elle s'engloutit dans mon ombre
Comme une pierre sur le ciel.

Elle a toujours les yeux ouverts
Et ne me laisse pas dormir.
Ses rêves en pleine lumière
Font s'évaporer les soleils,
Me font rire, pleurer et rire,
Parler sans avoir rien à dire.

(Mourir de ne pas mourir, 1924)

Lady Love

She is standing on my lids
And her hair is in my hair,
She has the colour of my eye,
She has the body of my hand,
In my shade she is engulfed
As a stone against the sky.

She will never close her eyes
And she does not let me sleep.
And her dreams in the bright day
Make the suns evaporate,
And me laugh cry and laugh,
Speak when I have nothing to say.

(Dying of not Dying, 1924)

A *perte de vue dans le sens de mon corps*

Tous les arbres toutes leurs branches toutes leurs feuilles
L'herbe à la base les rochers et les maisons en masse
Au loin la mer que ton oeil baigne
Ces images d'un jour après l'autre
Les vices les vertus tellement imparfaits
La transparence des passants dans les rues de hasard
Et les passantes exhalées par tes recherches obstinées
Tes idées fixes au coeur de plomb aux lèvres vierges
Les vices les vertus tellement imparfaits
La ressemblance des regards de permission avec les yeux
                                        que tu conquis
La confusion des corps des lassitudes des ardeurs
L'imitation des mots des attitudes des idées
Les vices les vertus tellement imparfaits

L'amour c'est l'homme inachevé.

Out of sight in the direction of my body

All the trees all their boughs all their leaves
The grass at the base the rocks the massed houses
Afar the sea that thine eye washes
Those images of one day and the next
The vices the virtues that are so imperfect
The transparence of men that pass in the streets of hazard
And women that pass in a fume from thy dour questing
The fixed ideas virgin-lipped leaden-hearted
The vices the virtues that are so imperfect
The eyes consenting resembling the eyes thou didst
                                                    vanquish
The confusion of the bodies the lassitudes the ardours
The imitation of the words the attitudes the ideas
The vices the virtues that are so imperfect

Love is man unfinished.

A *peine défigurée*

Adieu tristesse
Bonjour tristesse
Tu es inscrite dans les lignes du plafond
Tu es inscrite dans les yeux que j'aime
Tu n'es pas tout à fait la misère
Car les lèvres les plus pauvres te dénoncent
Par un sourire
Bonjour tristesse
Amour des corps aimables
Puissance de l'amour
Dont l'amabilité surgit
Comme un monstre sans corps
Tête désappointée
Tristesse beau visage.

(La Vie immédiate, 1932)

Scarcely disfigured

Farewell sadness
Greeting sadness
Thou art inscribed in the lines of the ceiling
Thou art inscribed in the eyes that I love
Thou art not altogether want
For the poorest lips denounce thee
Smiling
Greeting sadness
Love of the bodies that are lovable
Mightiness of love that lovable
Starts up as a bodiless beast
Head of hope defeated
Sadness countenance of beauty

(The Immediate Life, 1932)

Seconde nature

En l'honneur des muets des aveugles des sourds
A la grande pierre noire sur les épaules
Les disparitions du monde sans mystère

Mais aussi pour les autres à l'appel des choses par leur nom
La brûlure de toutes les métamorphoses
La chaîne entière des aurores dans la tête
Tous les cris qui s'acharnent à briser les mots

Et qui creusent la bouche et qui creusent les yeux
Où les couleurs furieuses défont les brumes de l'attente
Dressent l'amour contre la vie les morts en rêvent
Les bas-vivants partagent les autres sont esclaves
De l'amour comme on peut l'être de la liberté.

(L'Amour la poésie, 1929)

Second nature

In honour of the dumb the blind the deaf
Shouldering the great black stone
The things of time passing simply away

But then for the others knowing things by their names
The sear of every metamorphosis
The unbroken chain of dawns in the brain
The implacable cries shattering words

Furrowing the mouth furrowing the eyes
Where furious colours dispel the mists of vigil
Set up love against life that the dead dream of
The low-living share the others are slaves
Of love as some are slaves of freedom.

(Love, Poetry, 1929)

La vue

à Benjamin Péret

A l'heure où apparaissent les premiers symptômes de
la viduité de l'esprit
On peut voir un nègre toujours le même
Dans une rue très passante arborer ostensiblement une
cravate rouge
Il est toujours coiffé du même chapeau beige
Il a le visage de la méchanceté il ne regarde personne
Et personne ne le regarde.

Je n'aime ni les routes ni les montagnes ni les forêts
Je reste froid devant les ponts
Leurs arches ne sont pas pour moi des yeux je ne me
promène pas sur des sourcils
Je me promène dans les quartiers où il y a le plus de
femmes
Et je ne m'intéresse alors qu'aux femmes
Le nègre aussi car à l'heure où l'ennui et la fatigue
Deviennent les maîtres et me font indifférent à mes désirs
A moi-même
Je le rencontre toujours
Je suis indifférent il est méchant
Sa cravate doit être en fer forgé peint au minium
Faux feu de forge
Mais s'il est là par méchanceté
Je ne le remarque que par désoeuvrement.

Scene

At the hour when the first symptoms of mental viduity
                              make themselves felt
A negro is to be seen always the same negro
In a main thoroughfare ostensibly swanking a red tie
He always sports the same beige hat
He has the features of spite he looks at no one
And no one looks at him.

I love neither roads nor mountains nor forests
Bridges leave me cold
I do not see their arches as eyes I am not in the habit
                              of walking on brows
I am in the habit of walking in quarters where there are
                              the most women
And then I am interested only in women
The negro also for at the hour when boredom and fatigue
Daunt and detach me from desires
Then I meet him always
I am detached he is spiteful
His tie is certainly wrought iron with a coat of red-lead
False forge fire
But whether or not he is there out of spite
It is certain that I only notice him for want of something
                              better to do

Un évident besoin de ne rien voir traîne les ombres
Mais le soir titubant quitte son nid
Qu'est-ce que ce signal ces signaux ces alarmes
On s'étonne pour la dernière fois
En s'en allant les femmes enlèvent leur chemise de lumière
De but en but un seul but nul ne demeure
Quand nous n'y sommes plus la lumière est seule.

Le grenier de carmin a des recoins de jade
Et de jaspe si l'œil s'est refusé la nacre
La bouche est la bouche du sang
Le sureau tend le cou pour le lait du couteau
Un silex a fait peur à la nuit orageuse
Le risque enfant fait trébucher l'audace
Des pierres sur le chaume des oiseaux sur les tuiles
Du feu dans les moissons dans les poitrines
Joue avec le pollen de l'haleine nocturne
Taillée au gré des vents l'eau fait l'éclaboussée
L'éclat du jour s'enflamme aux courbes de la vague
Et dans son corset noir une morte séduit
Les scarabées de l'herbe et des branchages morts.

Parmi tant de passants.

(La Vie immédiate, 1932)

The shadows are yoked to an obvious determination to
see nothing
But forth from its nest the evening staggers
What is that signal those signals those alarms
It is the last astonishment of the evening
The women departing slip off their chemise of light
All of a single sudden not a soul remains
When we are gone the light is alone.

The carmine loft has nooks of jade
And jasper if the eye shuns nacre
The mouth is the mouth of the blood the elder
Cranes its neck for the milk of the blade
A flint has cowed the tempestuous night
Risk infant trips up daring
Stones on the stubble birds on the tiles
Fire in the harvests in the breasts
Playing with the pollen of the breath of the night
Hewn at the hands of the winds the water
Catches up her skirts and the scrolls of wave
Set the spark of dawn aflame
And in her black bodice a corpse seduces
The scarabs of the grass and of the dead boughs.

In a so thoroughfare.

(The Immediate Life, 1932)

L'Univers-Solitude

1
Une femme chaque nuit
Voyage en grand secret.

2
Villages de la lassitude
Où les filles ont les bras nus
Comme des jets d'eau
La jeunesse grandit en elles
Et rit sur la pointe des pieds.
Villages de la lassitude
Où tous les êtres sont pareils.

3
Pour voir les yeux où l'on s'enferme
Et les rires où l'on prend place.

4
Je veux t'embrasser je t'embrasse
Je veux te quitter tu t'ennuies
Mais aux limites de nos forces
Tu revêts une armure plus dangereuse qu'une arme.

Universe-Solitude

1
A woman every night
Journeys secretly.

2
Villages of weariness
Where the arms of girls are bare
As jets of water
Where their youth increasing in them
Laughs and laughs and laughs on tiptoe.
Villages of weariness
Where everybody is the same.

3
To see the eyes that cloister you
And the laughter that receives you.

4
I want to kiss thee I do kiss thee
I want to leave thee thou art tired
But when our strengths are at the ebb
Thou puttest on an armour more perilous than an arm.

5
Le corps et les honneurs profanes
Incroyable conspiration
Des angles doux comme des ailes.

— Mais la main qui me caresse
C'est mon rire qui l'ouvre
C'est ma gorge qui la retient
Qui la supprime.

Incroyable conspiration
Des découvertes et des surprises.

6
Fantôme de ta nudité
Fantôme enfant de ta simplicité
Dompteur puéril sommeil charnel
De libertés imaginaires.

7
A ce souffle à ce soleil d'hier
Qui joint tes lèvres
Cette caresse toute fraîche
Pour courir les mers légères de ta pudeur
Pour en façonner dans l'ombre
Les miroirs de jasmin
Le problème du calme.

5
The body and the profane honours
Incredible conspiracy
Of the angles soft as wings.

But the hand caressing me
It is my laughter that unclasps it
It is my throat that clings to it
That ends it.

Incredible conspiracy
Of the discoveries and surprises.

6
Phantom of thy nudity
Phantom child of thy simplicity
Child victor carnal sleep
Of unreal liberties.

7
It is the breath the yestersun
Joining thy lips
And it is the caress the fresh caress
To scour the frail seas of thy shame
To fashion them in gloom
It is the mirrors of jasmine
The problem of calm.

8
Désarmée
Elle ne se connaît plus d'ennemis.

9
Elle s'allonge
Pour se sentir moins seule.

10
J'admirais descendant vers toi
L'espace occupé par le temps
Nos souvenirs me transportaient

Il te manque beaucoup de place
Pour être toujours avec moi.

11
Déchirant ses baisers et ses peurs
Elle s'éveille la nuit
Pour s'étonner de tout ce qui l'a remplacée.

8
Disarmed
She knows of no enemy.

9
She stretches herself
That she may feel less alone.

10
I admired descending upon thee
Time in the chariot of space
Our memories transported me

Much room is denied thee
For ever with me.

11
Rending her kisses and her fears
She wakes in the night
To wonder at all that has replaced her.

Confections

1
La simplicité même écrire
Pour aujourd'hui la main est là.

2
Il faut voir de près
Les curieux
Quand on s'ennuie.

3
La violence des vents du large
Des navires de vieux visages
Une demeure permanente
Et des armes pour se défendre
Une plage peu fréquentée
Un coup de feu un seul
Stupéfaction du père
Mort depuis longtemps.

4
Tous ces gens mangent
Ils sont gourmands ils sont contents
Et s'ils rient ils mangent plus.

Confections

1
Simplicity yea even to write
To-day at least the hand is there.

2
It is meet to scrutinize
The inquisitive
When one is weary.

3
The violence of sea-winds
Ships old faces
A permanent abode
Weapons to defend one
A secluded shore
A shot one only
Stupefaction of the father
Dead this long time.

4
All these people eat
They are gluttonous they are happy
The more they laugh the more they eat.

5

Par-dessus les chapeaux
Un régiment d'orfraies passe au galop
C'est un régiment de chaussures
Toutes les collections des fétichistes déçus
Allant au diable.

6

Des cataclysmes d'or bien acquis
Et d'argent mal acquis.

7

Les oiseaux parfument les bois
Les rochers leurs grands lacs nocturnes.

8

Gagner au jeu du profil
Qu'un oiseau reste dans ses ailes.

9

Immobile
J'habite cette épine et ma griffe se pose
Sur les seins délicieux de la misère et du crime.

5
Above the hats
A regiment of ospreys gallops past
It is a regiment of shoes
All the disillusioned fetishists and their complete collections
Off to the devil.

6
Cataclysms of gold well-gotten
And of silver ill-gotten.

7
The birds perfume the woods
The rocks their great nocturnal lakes.

8
Play at profile and win
Let a bird abide in its wings.

9
Rapt
I dwell in this thorn and my claw alights
On the sweet breasts of poverty and crime.

10

Pourquoi les fait-on courir
On ne les fait pas courir
L'arrivée en avance
Le départ en retard

Quel chemin en arrière
Quand la lenteur s'en mêle.

Les preuves du contraire
Et l'inutilité.

11

Une limaille d'or un trésor une flaque
De platine au fond d'une vallée abominable
Dont les habitants n'ont plus de mains
Entraîne les joueurs à sortir d'eux-mêmes.

12

Le salon à la langue noire lèche son maître
Il l'embaume il lui tient lieu d'éternité.

13

Le passage de la Bérésina par une femme rousse à grandes
mamelles.

14

Il la prend dans ses bras
Lueurs brillantes un instant entrevues
Aux omoplates aux épaules aux seins
Puis cachées par un nuage.

Elle porte la main à son cœur
Elle pâlit elle frissonne
Qui donc a crié?

Mais l'autre s'il est encore vivant
On le retrouvera
Dans une ville inconnue.

10
Why are they made to run
They are not made to run
Arriving underdue
Departing overdue

What a road back
When slowness takes a hand.

Proofs of the contrary
And futility.

11
Gold-filings a treasure a platinum
Puddle deep in a horrible valley
Whose denizens have lost their hands
It takes the players out of themselves.

12
The drawing-room with its black tongue licks its master
Embalms him performs the office of eternity.

13
The Beresina forded by a sandy jug-dugged woman.

14
He takes her in his arms
Bright gleams for a second playing
On the shoulder-blades the shoulders and the breasts
Then hidden by a cloud.

She carries her hand to her heart
She pales she quakes
Whose then was the cry?

But he if he still lives
He shall be rediscovered
In a strange town.

15
Le sang coulant sur les dalles
Me fait des sandales
Sur une chaise au milieu de la rue
J'observe les petites filles créoles
Qui sortent de l'école en fumant la pipe.

16
Il ne faut pas voir la réalité telle que je suis.

17
Toute la vie a coulé dans mes rides
Comme une agate pour modeler
Le plus beau des masques funèbres.

18
Les arbres blancs les arbres noirs
Sont plus jeunes que la nature
Il faut pour retrouver ce hasard de naissance
Vieillir.

19
Soleil fatal du nombre des vivants
On ne conserve pas ton cœur.

(A toute épreuve, 1930)

15
The blood flowing on the flags
Furnishes me with sandals
I sit on a chair in the middle of the street
I observe the little Creole girls
Coming out of school smoking pipes.

16
Do not see reality as I am.

17
All life even as an agate has poured itself
Into the seams of my countenance and cast
A death-mask of unrivalled beauty.

18
The black trees the white trees
Are younger than nature
In order to recover this freak of birth one must
Age.

19
Fatal sun of the quick
One cannot keep thy heart.

(All Proof, 1930)

3. ARTHUR RIMBAUD

Le Bateau ivre

Comme je descendais des Fleuves impassibles,
Je ne me sentis plus guidé par les haleurs:
Des Peaux-Rouges criards les avaient pris pour cibles,
Les ayant cloués nus aux poteaux de couleurs.

J'étais insoucieux de tous les équipages,
Porteur de blés flamands ou de cotons anglais.
Quand avec mes haleurs ont fini ces tapages,
Les fleuves m'ont laissé descendre où je voulais.

Drunken Boat

Downstream on impassive rivers suddenly
I felt the towline of the boatmen slacken.
Redskins had taken them in a scream and stripped them and
Skewered them to the glaring stakes for targets.

Then, delivered from my straining boatmen,
From the trivial racket of trivial crews and from
The freights of Flemish grain and English cotton,
I made my own course down the passive rivers.

Dans les clapotements furieux des marées,
Moi, l'autre hiver, plus sourd que les cerveaux d'enfants,
Je courus! et les Péninsules démarrées
N'ont pas subi tohu-bohus plus triomphants.

La tempête a béni mes éveils maritimes.
Plus léger qu'un bouchon j'ai dansé sur les flots
Qu'on appelle rouleurs éternels de victimes,
Dix nuits, sans regretter l'œil niais des falots!

Plus douce qu'aux enfants la chair des pommes sures,
L'eau verte pénétra ma coque de sapin
Et des taches de vins bleus et des vomissures
Me lava, dispersant gouvernail et grappin.

Et dès lors, je me suis baigné dans le Poème
De la Mer, infusé d'astres, et lactescent,
Dévorant les azurs verts; où, flottaison blême
Et ravie, un noyé pensif, parfois descend;

Blanker than the brain of a child I fled
Through winter, I scoured the furious jolts of the tides,
In an uproar and a chaos of Peninsulas,
Exultant, from their moorings in triumph torn.

I started awake to tempestuous hallowings.
Nine nights I danced like a cork on the billows, I danced
On the breakers, sacrificial, for ever and ever,
And the crass eye of the lanterns was expunged.

More firmly bland than to children apples' firm pulp,
Soaked the green water through my hull of pine,
Scattering helm and grappling and washing me
Of the stains, the vomitings and blue wine.

Thenceforward, fused in the poem, milk of stars,
Of the sea, I coiled through deeps of cloudless green,
Where, dimly, they come swaying down,
Rapt and sad, singly, the drowned;

Où, teignant tout à coup les bleuités, délires
Et rhythmes lents sous les rutilements du jour,
Plus fortes que l'alcool, plus vastes que vos lyres,
Fermentent les rousseurs amères de l'amour!

Je sais les cieux crevant en éclairs, et les trombes
Et les ressacs et les courants: je sais le soir,
L'Aube exaltée ainsi qu'un peuple de colombes,
Et j'ai vu quelquefois ce que l'homme a cru voir!

J'ai vu le soleil bas, taché d'horreurs mystiques
Illuminant de longs figements violets,
Pareils à des acteurs de drames très antiques
Les flots roulant au loin leurs frissons de volets!

J'ai rêvé la nuit verte aux neiges éblouies,
Baiser montant aux yeux des mers avec lenteur,
La circulation des sèves inouïes,
Et l'éveil jaune et bleu des phosphores chanteurs!

Where, under the sky's haemorrhage, slowly tossing
In thuds of fever, arch-alcohol of song,
Pumping over the blues in sudden stains,
The bitter rednesses of love ferment.

I know the heavens split with lightnings and the currents
Of the sea and its surgings and its spoutings; I know evening,
And dawn exalted like a cloud of doves.
And my eyes have fixed phantasmagoria.

I have seen, as shed by ancient tragic footlights,
Out from the horror of the low sun's mystic stains,
Long weals of violet creep across the sea
And peals of ague rattle down its slats.

I have dreamt the green night's drifts of dazzled snow,
The slow climb of kisses to the eyes of the seas,
The circulation of unheard saps,
And the yellow-blue alarum of phosphors singing.

J'ai suivi, des mois pleins, pareille aux vacheries
Hystériques, la houle à l'assaut des récifs,
Sans songer que les pieds lumineux des Maries
Pussent forcer le muffle aux Océans poussifs !

J'ai heurté, savez-vous, d'incroyables Florides
Mêlant aux fleurs des yeux de panthères à peaux
D'hommes, des arcs-en-ciel tendus comme des brides
Sous l'horizon des mers, à de glauques troupeaux !

J'ai vu fermenter les marais, énormes nasses
Où pourrit dans les joncs tout un Léviathan,
Des écroulements d'eaux au milieu des bonaces
Et les lointains vers les gouffres cataractant !

Glaciers, soleils d'argent, flots nacreux, cieux de braises,
Échouages hideux au fond des golfes bruns
Où les serpents géants dévorés des punaises
Choient, des arbres tordus, avec de noirs parfums !

I have followed months long the maddened herds of the surf
Storming the reefs, mindless of the feet,
The radiant feet of the Marys that constrain
The stampedes of the broken-winded Oceans.

I have fouled, be it known, unspeakable Floridas, tangle of
The flowers of the eyes of panthers in the skins of
Men and the taut rainbows curbing,
Beyond the brows of the seas, the glaucous herds.

I have seen Leviathan sprawl rotting in the reeds
Of the great seething swamp-nets;
The calm sea disembowelled in waterslides
And the cataracting of the doomed horizons.

Iridescent waters, glaciers, suns of silver, flagrant skies,
And dark creeks' secret ledges, horror-strewn,
Where giant reptiles, pullulant with lice,
Lapse with dark perfumes from the writhing trees.

J'aurais voulu montrer aux enfants ces dorades
Du flot bleu, ces poissons d'or, ces poissons chantants.
Des écumes de fleurs ont béni mes dérades,
Et d'ineffables vents m'ont ailé par instants.

Parfois, martyr lassé des pôles et des zones,
La mer, dont le sanglot faisait mon roulis doux,
Montait vers moi ses fleurs d'ombre aux ventouses jaunes
Et je restais, ainsi qu'une femme à genoux...

Presque'île, ballottant sur mes bords les querelles
Et les fientes d'oiseaux clabaudeurs aux yeux blonds.
Et je voguais, lorsqu'à travers mes liens frêles
Des noyés descendaient dormir, à reculons!...

Or moi, bateau perdu sous les cheveux des anses,
Jeté par l'ouragan dans l'éther sans oiseau,
Moi dont les Monitors et les voiliers des Hanses
N'auraient pas repêché la carcasse ivre d'eau;

I would have shown to children those dorados
Of the blue wave, those golden fish, those singing fish;
In spumes of flowers I have risen from my anchors
And canticles of wind have blessed my wings.

Then toward me, rocking softly on its sobbing,
Weary of the torment of the poles and zones,
The sea would lift its yellow polyps on flowers
Of gloom and hold me—like a woman kneeling—

A stranded sanctuary for screeching birds,
Flaxen-eyed, shiteing on my trembling decks,
Till down they swayed to sleep, the drowned, spreadeagled,
And, sundering the fine tendrils, floated me.

Now I who was wrecked in the inlets' tangled hair
And flung beyond birds aloft by the hurricane,
Whose carcass drunk with water Monitors
And Hanseatic sloops could not have salved;

Libre, fumant, monté de brumes violettes,
Moi qui trouais le ciel rougeoyant comme un mur
Qui porte, confiture exquise aux bons poètes,
Des lichens de soleil et des morves d'azur;

Qui courais, taché de lunules électriques,
Planche folle, escorté des hippocampes noirs,
Quand les juillets faisaient crouler à coups de triques
Les cieux ultramarins aux ardents entonnoirs;

Moi qui tremblais, sentant geindre à cinquante lieues
Le rut des Béhémots et des Maelstroms épais,
Fileur éternel des immobilités bleues,
Je regrette l'Europe aux anciens parapets!

J'ai vu des archipels sidéraux! et des îles
Dont les cieux délirants sont ouverts au vogueur:
—Est-ce en ces nuits sans fond que tu dors et t'exiles,
Million d'oiseaux d'or, ô future Vigueur? —

Who, reeking and free in a fume of purple spray,
Have pierced the skies that flame as a wall would flame
For a chosen poet's rapture, and stream and flame
With solar lichen and with azure snot;

Who scudded, with my escort of black sea-horses,
Fury of timber, scarred with electric moons,
When Sirius flogged into a drift of ashes
The furnace-cratered cobalt of the skies;

I who heard in trembling across a waste of leagues
The turgent Stroms and Behemoths moan their rut,
I weaving for ever voids of spellbound blue,
Now remember Europe and her ancient ramparts.

I saw archipelagoes of stars and islands launched me
Aloft on the deep delirium of their skies:
Are these the fathomless nights of your sleep and exile,
Million of golden birds, oh Vigour to be?

Mais, vrai, j'ai trop pleuré! Les Aubes sont navrantes.
Toute lune est atroce et tout soleil amer:
L'âcre amour m'a gonflé de torpeurs enivrantes.
O que ma quille éclate! O que j'aille à la mer!

Si je désire une eau d'Europe, c'est la flache
Noire et froide où vers le crépuscule embaumé
Un enfant accroupi, plein de tristesse, lâche
Un bateau frêle comme un papillon de mai.

Je ne puis plus, baigné de vos langueurs, ô lames,
Enlever leur sillage aux porteurs de cotons,
Ni traverser l'orgueil des drapeaux et des flammes,
Ni nager sous les yeux horribles des pontons.

But no more tears. Dawns have broken my heart,
And every moon is torment, every sun bitterness;
I am bloated with the stagnant fumes of acrid loving—
May I split from stem to stern and founder, ah founder!

I want none of Europe's waters unless it be
The cold black puddle where a child, full of sadness,
Squatting, looses a boat as frail
As a moth into the fragrant evening.

Steeped in the languors of the swell, I may
Absorb no more the wake of the cotton-freighters,
Nor breast the arrogant oriflammes and banners,
Nor swim beneath the leer of the pontoons.

4. GUILLAUME APOLLINAIRE

Zone

A la fin tu es las de ce monde ancien

Bergère ô tour Eiffel le troupeau des ponts bêle ce matin

Tu en as assez de vivre dans l'antiquité grecque et romaine

Ici même les automobiles ont l'air d'être anciennes
La religion seule est restée toute neuve la religion
Est restée simple comme les hangars de Port-Aviation

Seul en Europe tu n'es pas antique ô Christianisme
L'Européen le plus moderne c'est vous Pape Pie X
Et toi que les fenêtres observent la honte te retient
D'entrer dans une église et de t'y confesser ce matin
Tu lis les prospectus les catalogues les affiches qui
                                        chantent tout haut
Voilà la poésie ce matin et pour la prose il y a les journaux
Il y a les livraisons à 25 centimes pleines d'aventures
                                        policières
Portraits des grands hommes et mille titres divers

Zone

In the end you are weary of this ancient world

This morning the bridges are bleating Eiffel Tower oh herd

Weary of living in Roman antiquity and Greek

Here even the motor-cars look antique
Religion alone has stayed young religion
Has stayed simple like the hangars at Port Aviation

You alone in Europe Christianity are not ancient
The most modern European is you Pope Pius X
And you whom the windows watch shame restrains
From entering a church this morning and confessing your
sins
You read the handbills the catalogues the singing posters
So much for poetry this morning and the prose is in
the papers
Special editions full of crimes
Celebrities and other attractions for 25 centimes

J'ai vu ce matin une jolie rue dont j'ai oublié le nom
Neuve et propre du soleil elle était le clairon
Les directeurs les ouvriers et les belles sténo-dactylographes
Du lundi matin au samedi soir quatre fois par jour y passent
Le matin par trois fois la sirène y gémit
Une cloche rageuse y aboie vers midi
Les inscriptions des enseignes et des murailles
Les plaques les avis à la façon des perroquets criaillent
J'aime la grâce de cette rue industrielle
Située à Paris entre la rue Aumont-Thiéville et l'avenue
                                        des Ternes

Voilà la jeune rue et tu n'es encore qu'un petit enfant
Ta mère ne t'habille que de bleu et de blanc
Tu es très pieux et avec le plus ancien de tes camarades
                                        René Dalize
Vous n'aimez rien tant que les pompes de l'Église
Il est neuf heures le gaz est baissé tout bleu vous sortez
                                        du dortoir en cachette
Vous priez toute la nuit dans la chapelle du collège
Tandis qu'éternelle et adorable profondeur améthyste
Tourne à jamais la flamboyante gloire du Christ
C'est le beau lys que tous nous cultivons
C'est la torche aux cheveux roux que n'éteint pas le vent
C'est le fils pâle et vermeil de la douloureuse mère
C'est l'arbre toujours touffu de toutes les prières
C'est la double potence de l'honneur et de l'éternité
C'est l'étoile à six branches
C'est Dieu qui meurt le vendredi et ressuscite le dimanche

This morning I saw a pretty street whose name is gone
Clean and shining clarion of the sun
Where from Monday morning to Saturday evening four
                                         times a day
Directors workers and beautiful shorthand typists go their
                                                    way
And thrice in the morning the siren makes its moan
And a bell bays savagely coming up to noon
The inscriptions on walls and signs
The notices and plates squawk parrot-wise
I love the grace of this industrial street
In Paris between the Avenue des Ternes and the Rue
                                         Aumont-Thiéville

There it is the young street and you still but a small child
Your mother always dresses you in blue and white
You are very pious and with René Dalize your oldest crony
Nothing delights you more than church ceremony
It is nine at night the lowered gas burns blue you steal away
From the dormitory and all night in the college chapel pray
Whilst everlastingly the flaming glory of Christ
Wheels in adorable depths of amethyst
It is the fair lily that we all revere
It is the torch burning in the wind its auburn hair
It is the rosepale son of the mother of grief
It is the tree with the world's prayers ever in leaf
It is of honour and eternity the double beam
It is the six-branched star it is God
Who Friday dies and Sunday rises from the dead

C'est le Christ qui monte au ciel mieux que les aviateurs
Il détient le record du monde pour la hauteur

Pupille Christ de l'œil
Vingtième pupille des siècles il sait y faire
Et changé en oiseau ce siècle comme Jésus monte dans l'air
Les diables dans les abîmes lèvent la tête pour le regarder
Ils disent qu'il imite Simon Mage en Judée
Ils crient s'il sait voler qu'on l'appelle voleur
Les anges voltigent autour du joli voltigeur
Icare Enoch Élie Apollonius de Thyane
Flottent autour du premier aéroplane
Ils s'écartent parfois pour laisser passer ceux que transporte
                                        la Sainte-Eucharistie
Ces prêtres qui montent éternellement élevant l'hostie
L'avion se pose enfin sans refermer les ailes
Le ciel s'emplit alors de millions d'hirondelles
A tire-d'aile viennent les corbeaux les faucons les hiboux
D'Afrique arrivent les ibis les flamants les marabouts
L'oiseau Roc célébré par les conteurs et les poètes
Plane tenant dans ses serres le crâne d'Adam la première tête
L'aigle fond de l'horizon en poussant un grand cri
Et d'Amérique vient le petit colibri
De Chine sont venus ses pihis longs et souples
Qui n'ont qu'une seule aile et qui volent par couples
Puis voici la colombe esprit immaculé
Qu'escortent l'oiseau-lyre et le paon ocellé
Le phénix ce bûcher qui soi-même s'engendre

It is Christ who better than airmen wings his flight
Holding the record of the world for height

Pupil Christ of the eye
Twentieth pupil of the centuries it is no novice
And changed into a bird this century soars like Jesus
The devils in the deeps look up and say they see a
Nimitation of Simon Magus in Judea
Craft by name by nature craft they cry
About the pretty flyer the angels fly
Enoch Elijah Apollonius of Tyana hover
With Icarus round the first airworthy ever
For those whom the Eucharist transports they now and
                                                    then make way
Host-elevating priests ascending endlessly
The aeroplane alights at last with outstretched pinions
Then the sky is filled with swallows in their millions
The rooks come flocking the owls the hawks
Flamingoes from Africa and ibises and storks
The roc bird famed in song and story soars
With Adam's skull the first head in its claws
The eagle stoops screaming from heaven's verge
From America comes the little humming-bird
From China the long and supple
One-winged peehees that fly in couples
Behold the dove spirit without alloy
That ocellate peacock and lyre-bird convoy
The phoenix flame-devoured flame-revived

Un instant voile tout de son ardente cendre
Les sirènes laissant les périlleux détroits
Arrivent en chantant bellement toutes trois
Et tous aigle phénix et pihis de la Chine
Fraternisent avec la volante machine

Maintenant tu marches dans Paris tout seul parmi la foule
Des troupeaux d'autobus mugissants près de toi roulent
L'angoisse de l'amour te serre le gosier
Comme si tu ne devais jamais plus être aimé
Si tu vivais dans l'ancien temps tu entrerais dans un
                                        monastère
Vous avez honte quand vous vous surprenez à dire une
                                        prière
Tu te moques de toi et comme le feu de l'Enfer ton rire
                                        pétille
Les étincelles de ton rire dorent le fond de ta vie
C'est un tableau pendu dans un sombre musée
Et quelquefois tu vas le regarder de près

Aujourd'hui tu marches dans Paris les femmes sont
                                        ensanglantées
C'était et je voudrais ne pas m'en souvenir c'était au
                                        déclin de la beauté

Entourée de flammes ferventes Notre-Dame m'a regardé
                                        à Chartres
Le sang de votre Sacré Coeur m'a inondé à Montmartre
Je suis malade d'ouïr les paroles bienheureuses
L'amour dont je souffre est une maladie honteuse
Et l'image qui te possède te fait survivre dans l'insomnie
                                        et dans l'angoisse
C'est toujours près de toi cette image qui passe

All with its ardent ash an instant hides
Leaving the perilous straits the sirens three
Divinely singing join the company
And eagle phoenix peehees fraternize
One and all with the machine that flies

Now you walk in Paris alone among the crowd
Herds of bellowing buses hemming you about
Anguish of love parching you within
As though you were never to be loved again
If you lived in olden times you would get you to a cloister
You are ashamed when you catch yourself at a paternoster
You are your own mocker and like hellfire your laughter
                                                    crackles
Golden on your life's hearth fall the sparks of your laughter
It is a picture in a dark museum hung
And you sometimes go and contemplate it long

To-day you walk in Paris the women are blood-red
It was and would I could forget it was at beauty's ebb

From the midst of fervent flames Our Lady beheld me
                                                at Chartres
The blood of your Sacred Heart flooded me in Montmartre
I am sick with hearing the words of bliss
The love I endure is like a syphilis
And the image that possesses you and never leaves your
                                                    side
In anguish and insomnia keeps you alive

Maintenant tu es au bord de la Méditerranée
Sous les citronniers qui sont en fleur toute l'année
Avec tes amis tu te promènes en barque
L'un est Nissard il y a un Mentonasque et deux
                                           Turbiasques
Nous regardons avec effroi les poulpes des profondeurs
Et parmi les algues nagent les poissons images du Sauveur

Tu es dans le jardin d'une auberge aux environs de Prague
Tu te sens tout heureux une rose est sur la table
Et tu observes au lieu d'écrire ton conte en prose
La cétoine qui dort dans le coeur de la rose

Épouvanté tu te vois dessiné dans les agates de Saint-Vit
Tu étais triste à mourir le jour où tu t'y vis
Tu ressembles au Lazare affolé par le jour
Les aiguilles de l'horloge du quartier juif vont à rebours
Et tu recules aussi dans ta vie lentement
En montant au Hradchin et le soir en écoutant
Dans les tavernes chanter des chansons tchèques

Te voici à Marseille au milieu des pastèques

Te voici à Coblence à l'hôtel du Géant

Te voici à Rome assis sous un néflier du Japon

Te voici à Amsterdam avec une jeune fille que tu trouves
                                      belle et qui est laide
Elle doit se marier avec un étudiant de Leyde

Now you are on the Riviera among
The lemon-trees that flower all year long
With your friends you go for a sail on the sea
One is from Nice one from Menton and two from La Turbie
The octopuses in the depths fill us with horror
And in the seaweed fishes swim emblems of the Saviour

You are in an inn-garden near Prague
You feel perfectly happy a rose is on the table
And you observe instead of writing your story in prose
The chafer asleep in the heart of the rose

Appalled you see your image in the agates of Saint Vitus
That day you were fit to die with sadness
You look like Lazarus frantic in the daylight
The hands of the clock in the Jewish quarter go to left
                                                    from right
And you too live slowly backwards
Climbing up to the Hradchin or listening as night falls
To Czech songs being sung in taverns

Here you are in Marseilles among the water-melons

Here you are in Coblenz at the Giant's Hostelry

Here you are in Rome under a Japanese medlar-tree

Here you are in Amsterdam with an ill-favoured maiden
You find her beautiful she is engaged to a student in
                                                    Leyden

On y loue des chambres en latin Cubicula locanda
Je m'en souviens j'y ai passé trois jours et autant à Gouda

Tu es à Paris chez le juge d'instruction
Comme un criminel on te met en état d'arrestation

Tu as fait de douloureux et de joyeux voyages
Avant de t'apercevoir du mensonge et de l'âge
Tu as souffert de l'amour à vingt et à trente ans
J'ai vécu comme un fou et j'ai perdu mon temps
Tu n'oses plus regarder tes mains et à tous moments
                                        je voudrais sangloter
Sur toi sur celle que j'aime sur tout ce qui t'a épouvanté

Tu regardes les yeux pleins de larmes ces pauvres émigrants
Ils croient en Dieu ils prient les femmes allaitent des enfants
Ils emplissent de leur odeur le hall de la gare Saint-Lazare
Ils ont foi dans leur étoile comme les rois-mages
Ils espèrent gagner de l'argent dans l'Argentine
Et revenir dans leur pays après avoir fait fortune
Une famille transporte un édredon rouge comme vous
                                        transportez votre coeur
Cet édredon et nos rêves sont aussi irréels
Quelques-uns de ces émigrants restent ici et se logent
Rue des Rosiers ou rue des Écouffes dans des bouges
Je les ai vus souvent le soir ils prennent l'air dans la rue
Et se déplacent rarement comme les pièces aux échecs
Il y a surtout des Juifs leurs femmes portent perruque
Elles restent assises exsangues au fond des boutiques

There they let their rooms in Latin cubicula locanda
I remember I spent three days there and as many in Gouda

You are in Paris with the examining magistrate
They clap you in gaol like a common reprobate

Grievous and joyous voyages you made
Before you knew what falsehood was and age
At twenty you suffered from love and at thirty again
My life was folly and my days in vain
You dare not look at your hands tears haunt my eyes
For you for her I love and all the old miseries

Weeping you watch the wretched emigrants
They believe in God they pray the women suckle their
                                                    infants
They fill with their smell the station of Saint-Lazare
Like the wise men from the East they have faith in their star
They hope to prosper in the Argentine
And to come home having made their fortune
A family transports a red eiderdown as you your heart
An eiderdown as unreal as our dreams
Some go no further doss in the stews
Of the Rue des Rosiers or the Rue des Ecouffes
Often in the streets I have seen them in the gloaming
Taking the air and like chessmen seldom moving
They are mostly Jews the wives wear wigs and in
The depths of shadowy dens bloodless sit on and on

Tu es debout devant le zinc d'un bar crapuleux
Tu prends un café à deux sous parmi les malheureux

Tu es la nuit dans un grand restaurant

Ces femmes ne sont pas méchantes elles ont des soucis
                                                    cependant
Toutes même la plus laide a fait souffrir son amant

Elle est la fille d'un sergent de ville de Jersey

Ses mains que je n'avais pas vues sont dures et gercées

J'ai une pitié immense pour les coutures de son ventre

J'humilie maintenant à une pauvre fille au rire horrible
                                                    ma bouche

Tu es seul le matin va venir
Les laitiers font tinter leurs bidons dans les rues

La nuit s'éloigne ainsi qu'une belle Métive
C'est Ferdine la fausse ou Léa l'attentive

Et tu bois cet alcool brûlant comme ta vie
Ta vie que tu bois comme une eau-de-vie

You stand at the bar of a crapulous café
Drinking coffee at two sous a time in the midst of the

                                        unhappy

It is night you are in a restaurant it is superior

These women are decent enough they have their troubles

                                 however
All even the ugliest one have made their lovers suffer

She is a Jersey police-constable's daughter

Her hands I had not seen are chapped and hard

The seams of her belly go to my heart

To a poor harlot horribly laughing I humble my mouth

You are alone morning is at hand
In the streets the milkmen rattle their cans

Like a dark beauty night withdraws
Watchful Leah or Ferdine the false

And you drink this alcohol burning like your life
Your life that you drink like spirit of wine

173

Tu marches vers Auteuil tu veux aller chez toi à pied
Dormir parmi tes fétiches d'Océanie et de Guinée
Ils sont des Christ d'une autre forme et d'une autre
                                                    croyance
Ce sont les Christ inférieurs des obscures espérances

Adieu Adieu

Soleil cou coupé

1913

You walk towards Auteuil you want to walk home and
                                                    sleep
Among your fetishes from Guinea and the South Seas
Christs of another creed another guise
The lowly Christs of dim expectancies

Adieu Adieu

Sun corseless head

1950

5. SÉBASTIEN CHAMFORT

Huit Maximes

Le sot qui a un moment d'esprit étonne et scandalise comme des chevaux de fiacre qui galopent.

Long after Chamfort

Wit in fools has something shocking
Like cabhorses galloping.

Le théâtre tragique a le grand inconvénient moral de mettre trop d'importance à la vie et à la mort.

The trouble with tragedy is the fuss it makes
About life and death and other tuppenny aches.

Quand on soutient que les gens les moins sensibles sont, hà tout prendre, les plus heureux, je me rappelle le proverbe indien: 'Il vaux mieux être assis que debout, couché qu'assis, mort que tout cela.'

Better on your arse than on your feet,
Flat on your back than either, dead than the lot.

Quand on a été bien tourmenté, bien fatigué par sa propre sensibilité, on s'aperçoit qu'il faut vivre au jour le jour, oublier beaucoup, enfin éponger la vie à mesure qu'elle s'écoule.

Live and clean forget from day to day,
Mop life up as fast as it dribbles away.

La pensée console de tout et remédie à tout. Si quelquefois elle vous fait du mal, demandez-lui le remède du mal qu'elle vous a fait, elle vous le donnera.

Ask of all-healing, all-consoling thought
Salve and solace for the woe it wrought.

L'espérance n'est qu'un charlatan qui nous trompe sans cesse; et, pour moi, le bonheur n'a commencé que lorsque je l'ai eu perdu. Je mettrais volontiers sur la porte du paradis le vers que le Dante a mis sur celle de l'enfer: *Lasciate ogni speranza etc.*

Hope is a knave befools us evermore,
Which till I lost no happiness was mine.
I strike from hell's to grave on heaven's door:
All hope abandon ye who enter in.

Vivre est une maladie dont le sommeil nous soulage toutes les seize heures. C'est un palliatif; la mort est le remède.

sleep till death
healeth
come ease
this life disease

Que le coeur de l'homme est creux et plein d'ordure.

how hollow heart and full
of filth thou art

PART IV

EARLY POEMS

Calvary by Night

the water
the waste of water

in the womb of water
an pansy leaps

rocket of bloom flare flower of night wilt for me
on the breasts of the water it has closed it has made
an act of floral presence on the water
the tranquil act of its cycle on the waste
from the spouting forth
to the re-enwombing
an untroubled bow of petal and fragrance
kingfished abated
drowned for me
Lamb of my insustenance

till the clamour of a blue flower
beat on the walls of the womb of
the waste of
the water

Casket Of Pralinen For A Daughter Of A Dissipated Mandarin

Is he long enough in the leg?
Già but his faice...
Oh me little timid Rosinette
isn't it Bartholo, synthetic grey cat, regal candle?
Keep Thyrsis for your morning ones.
Hold your head well over the letter darling
or they'll fall on the blotting.
Will you ever forget that soupe arrosée
on the first of the first,
spoonfeeding the weeping gladiator
renewing our baptismal vows
and dawn cracking all along the line
Slobbery assumption of the innocents
two Irish in one God.

Radiant lemon-whiskered Christ
and you obliging porte-phallic-portfolio
and blood-faced Tom
disbelieving
in the Closerie cocktail that is my
and of course John the bright boy of the class
swallowing an apostolic spit
THE BULLIEST FEED IN 'ISTORY
if the boy scouts hadn't booked a trough
for the eleventh's eleventh eleven years after.

Now me boy
take a hitch in your lyrical loinstring.
What is this that is more
than the anguish of Beauty,

this gale of pain that was not prepared
in the caves of her eyes?

Is it enough
a stitch in the hem of the garment of God?

To-night her gaze would be less
than a lark's barred sunlight.

Oh I am ashamed
of all clumsy artistry
I am ashamed of presuming
to arrange words
of everything but the ingenuous fibres
that suffer honestly.

Fool! do you hope to untangle
the knot of God's pain?

Melancholy Christ that was a soft one!
Oh yes I think that was perhaps just a very little
    inclined to be rather too self-conscious.

Schluss!
Now ladies and gents
a chocolate-coated hiccough to our old friend.
Put on your hats and sit easy.
Oh beauty!
oh thou predatory evacuation,
from the bowels of my regret—
readily affected

by the assimilation of a purging gobbet
from my memory's involuntary vomit—
violently projected,
oh beauty!
oh innocent and spluttering beautiful!

What price the Balbec express?
Albion Albion mourn for him mourn
thy cockerup Willy the idiot boy
the portly scullion's codpiece.
Now who'll discover in Mantegna's
butchery stout foreshortened Saviour
recognitions of transcendent
horse-power?
Sheep he wrote the very much doubting
genial illegible landscape gardener.
Gloucester's no bimbo
and he's in Limbo
so all's well with the gorgonzola cheese of human
    kindness.

Though the swine were slaughtered
beneath the waves
not far from the firm sand
they're gone they're gone
my Brussels Braut!

SONNET

At last I find in my confusèd soul,
Dark with the dark flame of the cypresses,
The certitude that I cannot be whole,
Consummate, finally achieved, unless

I be consumed and fused in the white heat
Of her sad finite essence, so that none
Shall sever us who are at last complete
Eternally, irrevocably one,

One with the birdless, cloudless, colourless skies,
One with the bright purity of the fire
of which we are and for which we must die
A rapturous strange death and be entire,

Like syzygetic stars, supernly bright,
Conjoined in One and in the Infinite!

TEXT

Miserere oh colon
oh passionate ilium
and Frances the cook in the study mourning
an abstract belly
instead of the writhing asparagus-plumer
smashed on delivery
by the most indifferential calculus
that never came out
or ever disdressed
a redknuckled slut of a Paduan Virtue.

Show that plate here to your bedfruit
spent baby
and take a good swig
at our buxom calabash.
There's more than bandit Glaxo
underneath me maternity toga.
So she sags and here's the other.

That's the real export or I'm a Jungfrau.
Now wipe your moustache and hand us the vaseline.

Open Thou my lips
and
(if one dare make a suggestion)
Thine eye of skyflesh.
Am I a token of Godcraft?
The masterpiece of a scourged apprentice?
Where is my hippopot's cedar tail?
and belly muscles?
Shall I cease to lament
being not as the flashsneezing

non-suppliant airtight alligator?
Not so but perhaps
at the sight and the sound of
a screechy flatfooted Tuscany peacock's
Strauss fandango and recitative
not forgetting
he stinks eternal.

Alas my scorned packthread!
No blade has smoothed the furrowed cheeks
that my tears corrode.
My varicose veins take my kneeling thoughts
from the piteous pelican.
Quick tip losers narcissistic inverts.
Twice I parted two crawlers
dribbling their not connubial strangles
in Arcadia of all places.
Believe me Miss Ops
swan flame or shower of gold
its one to ten at the time
(no offence to your noble deathjerks)
I know I was at it seven...
the bitch she's blinded me!
Manto me dear
an iced sherbet and me blood's a solid.

We are proud in our pain
our life was not blind.

Worms breed in their red tears
as they slouch by unnamed
scorned by the black ferry
despairing of death
who shall not scour in swift joy
the bright hill's girdle
nor tremble with the dark pride of torture
and the bitter dignity of an ingenious damnation.
Lo-Ruhama Lo-Ruhama
pity is quick with death.
Presumptuous passionate fool come now
to the sad maimed shades
and stand cold
on the cold moon.

FOR FUTURE REFERENCE

My cherished chemist friend
lured me aloofly
down from the cornice
into the basement
and there:
drew bottles of acid and alkali out of his breast
to a colourscale accompaniment
    (mad dumbells spare me!)
fiddling deft and expert
with the doubled jointed nutcrackers of the hen's ovaries
But I stilled my cringing
and smote him
yes oh my strength!
smashed
mashed
    (peace my incisors!)
flayed and crushed him
with a ready are you steady
cuff-discharge.
But did I?

And then the bright waters
beneath the broad board
the trembling blade of the streamlined divers
and down to our waiting
to my enforced buoyancy
came floating the words of
the Mutilator
and the work of his fingerjoints:
observe gentlemen one of

the consequences of the displacement of
  (click)!
the muncher.
The hair shall be grey
above the left temple
the hair shall be grey there
  abracadabra!
  sweet wedge of birds faithless!
God blast you yes it is we see
God bless you professor
we can't clap or we'd sink
three cheers for the perhaps pitiful professor
next per shaving? next per sh. . . . . . . ?
Well of all the . . . . . !
that little bullet-headed bristle-cropped
red-faced rat of a pure mathematician
that I thought was experimenting with barbed wire in
  the Punjab
up he comes surging to the landing steps
and tells me I'm putting no guts in my kick.
Like this he says like this.
Well I just swam out nimbly
blushing and hopeless
with the little swift strokes that I like and . . . . .
Whoops!
over the stream and the tall green bank
in a strong shallow arch
and his face all twisted calm and patient
and the board ledge doing its best to illustrate
Bruno's identification of contraries
into the water or on to the stones?

No matter at all he can't come back
from far bay or stony ground
yes here he is
(he must have come under)
for the second edition
    coming
house innings set half or anything . . .

if he can't come twice
or forgets his lesson
or breaks his leg
he might forget me
they all might . . . . . !

so the snowy floor of the parrot's cell
burning at dawn
the palaiate of my strange mouth.

HELL CRANE TO STARLING

Oholiba charm of my eyes
there is a cave above Tsoar
and a Spanish donkey there.

You needn't bring wine to that non-relation.

And he won't know
who changed his name
when Jehovah sprained the seam of his haunch
in Peniel in Peniel
after he's sent on the thirty camels
suckling for dear death
and so many fillies
that I don't want log tablets.

Mister Jacobson mister Hippolitus-in-hell Jacobson
we all know
how you tried to rejoin your da.
Bilha always blabs.

Because Benoni skirted aftercrop
of my aching loins
you'll never see him
reddening the wall in two dimensions
and if you did
you might spare the postage to Chaldea.

But there's a bloody fine ass
lepping with stout and impurée de pommes
in the hill above Tsoar.

FROM THE ONLY POET TO A SHINING WHORE

For Henry Crowder to sing.

Rahab of the holy battlements,
bright dripping shaft
in the bright bright patient
pearl-brow dawn-dusk lover of the sun.

Puttanina mia!
You hid them happy in the high flax,
pale before the fords
of Jordan, and the dry red waters,
and you lowered a pledge
of scarlet hemp.

Oh radiant, oh angry, oh Beatrice,
she foul with the victory
of the bloodless fingers
and proud, and you, Beatrice, mother, sister,
    daughter, belovèd,
fierce pale flame
of doubt, and God's sorrow,
and my sorrow.

RETURN TO THE VESTRY

Lover
off with your braces
Slouch in unbuttoned ease
fill a sack take a porter climb a mountain
as he did
the deaf conceited lecherous laypriest
the vindictive old sausage-sprinkler
dirt in a dirt floor
in a chapel barn
by a stifled stream.
Zoroaster
politely factorized
and a hay-rake
guarantee his siesta
except during the harvest season when the
    latter is removed.
I may be mistaken
but—
tears covering all risks—
I took a time exposure
and wept into my hat
So
swell the cairn and spill the doings.
Burn sulphur!
Juniper flame to a swirl of ashes!
Drown the Singer
I'm done with stitch anguish.

Now a compress of wormwood and verbena
on my fiery buttocks
Smother the place in Cerebos it stinks of breeding.
Here's the mange of beauty in a corporation bucket!
Shovel it into the winds!
Loose the sparrows.
Pluck that pigeon she dribbles fertility.
Mumps and a orchid to Fräulein Miranda.
Gentle Anteros
dark and dispassionate
come a grave snake with peace to my quarry
and choke my regret
noble Anteros
and coil at the door of my quarry tomb
and span its rim with a luminous awning
shallow and dim
as a grey tilt of silk
filtering sadly
the weary triumph of morning.

Or mock a duller impurity.

YOKE OF LIBERTY

The lips of her desire are grey
and parted like a silk loop
threatening
a slight wanton wound.
She preys wearily
on sensitive wild things
proud to be torn
by the grave crouch of her beauty.
But she will die and her snare
tendered so patiently
to my tamed watchful sorrow
will break and hang
in a pitiful crescent.

TAILPIECE

Tailpiece

who may tell the tale
of the old man?
weigh absence in a scale?
mete want with a span?
the sum assess
of the world's woes?
nothingness
in words enclose?

NOTES

PART ONE

Whoroscope
Written as an entry for the Nancy Cunard £10 Competition for the best poem on the subject of Time in the Summer of 1930, which it won. The judges were Nancy Cunard and Richard Aldington. The original edition consisted of 100 signed and 200 unsigned copies published by Nancy Cunard's Hours Press. One condition of the Competition was that the poem should be no more than 100 lines. The Notes were added later at the suggestion of Richard Aldington. The poem is based on Adrien Baillet's late 17th century life of Descartes. It is Descartes speaking.

Gnome
First published in the *Dublin Magazine* IX (July–September 1934) Inspired by Goethe's *Xenien*.

Home Olga
First published in *Contempo* (Chapel Hill N.C.) III, No 13 (February 15, 1934). The poem is an obscure acrostic on the name of Joyce, composed for a special Joycean occasion, which may have been Bloomsday 1932. The title is a euphemism for '*foutons le camp d'ici*', which was freely used by Tom MacGreevy and his friends.

The Vulture
Based on a fragment from Goethe's *Harzreise in Winter.*

Enueg I and *II*
Written in the form of a Provençal dirge or lament. The poet at the time was a lecturer at Trinity College.

Alba
Written about the same time as the above, and also based on a Provençal model. Alba is the dawn which lovers dread, as they must separate when it breaks. First appeared *Dublin Magazine* VI (Oct–Dec 1931).

Dortmunder
Written in Kassel. The title is taken from the German beer.

Sanies I and *II*
The first poem is set in Dublin, the second in Paris. Both are also based on Provençal models. The title is Latin for 'morbid discharge'.

Serena I, II and *III*
Again the models are Provençal, based on Troubadour evening poems.
Thales (line 2) took a pantheistic view of the soul ('all things full of Gods').

Malacoda
Written after the death of the poet's father from a heart attack in 1933. In
Dante, Malacoda is a deceitful demon.

Da Tagte Es
Also written after the death of the poet's father. Compare Walther von der
Vogelweide's *Nemt, frowe, disen kranz* of which the last line of the second to last
stanza reads *do taget ez und muoso ich wachen.*

Echo's Bones
Title taken from Ovid's Metamorphoses iii, 341–401.
The whole cycle of poems was published in 1935 by Europa Press (George
Reavey) and was No. 3 in the series Europa Poets. The original title was
Echo's Bones and Other Precipitates.

Cascando
First published in the *Dublin Magazine* XI (Oct.-Dec. 1936). Line 4 originally
read *is it better abort than be barren* and was the first line. The first three lines
and the addition of *not* is a later version.

Ooftish
First published in *Transition: Tenth Anniversary* (April–May 1938). The title is a
Yiddish expression meaning 'put your money down on the table.'

Saint-Lô
Written in 1946 and first published in the *Irish Times* June 24 that year.
Originally in five lines with lines 3 and 4 as follows:
and the old mind / ghost-abandoned

Song
This poem appears in *Words and Music* (Faber & Faber) and is sung by Words
in the play written for BBC radio and first broadcast on 13th February 1962.

Antipepsis
Unpublished poem from the Beckett Archive at Reading University, dated
by the author *after St. Lo 1946.* The office of the Irish Censorship was then in
St. Stephen's Green in Dublin. Reputedly it was in response to the banning
of *More Pricks than Kicks* in the late thirties, but the poem may have been
revised later.

The Downs
This poem first appeared in *The Sunday Times* shortly before Beckett's death. When asked by the editor, Beckett could not remember when he had written it, but said that it came to him when looking down at the Thames from Waterloo Bridge. One possibility is therefore that it dates from the time in 1964 when he attended rehearsals at the National Theatre for *Play*, when he first met Billie Whitelaw.

Something there
First published in *New Departures*, Special Issue No 7/8 and 10/11 1975. Compare to *hors crâne*.

Late Poems (Mirlitonnades)
Samuel Beckett, often sitting alone in cafés, would make little notes, arrangement of words, phrases that occurred to him, many to be incorporated into work on which he was engaged, and little poems, sometime written on beer mats. Many of these have appeared as *Mirlitonnades* or 'bird calls' in the last edition of the *Collected Poems*. More are included in this volume, mostly taken from his notebooks and Commonplace Book which he gave to the Reading archive, into which he copied them. The previously unpublished French mirlitonnades start on page 105.

Go where never before and *Brief Dream* were sent respectively to James Knowlson, his biographer, and John Calder his publisher, by the author in 1989.

The Notes to Part I were compiled by the publishers with reference to *Samuel Beckett: His Works and His Critics* by Raymond Federman and John Fletcher. (Univ. of California Press 1970). James Knowlson and the author also contributed information.

PART TWO

elles viennent
Originally written in English in 1937 and translated into French by the author before 1946. The English text is given by Peggy Guggenheim in her memoirs (Out of This Century, New York 1946 page 205 on) and differs slightly from the French version (the last line containing *life* where one would expect *love*) in the Guggenheim book. In this volume Mr. Beckett has changed *life* back to *love*. The French version appeared for the first time in *Les Temps Modernes* Volume Two No. 14. (November 1946).

à elle l'acte calme
Written between 1937 and 1939, this poem appeared for the first time in *Les Temps Modernes* (as above).

jusque dans la caverne ciel et sol
Written in the same period and first published in *Les Temps Modernes* (as above).

bon bon il est un pays
Written between 1947 and 1949 and appeared for the first time in *Les Cahiers des Saisons* No. 2 (October 1955) under the title *Accul*. Line 18 originally started with a capital letter.

Mort de A.D.
Poem written about 1947 in memory of a colleague at the Irish Red Cross Hospital in Saint-Lô (Manche), which appeared for the first time in *Les Cahiers des Saisons* (as above). The second last line originally read *vieux bois grêlé témoin des départs*.

vive morte ma seule saison
Date and publication as above.

je suis ce cours de sable qui glisse
Written in 1948 and published for the first time in *Transition Forty-Eight* No. 2 (June 1948 page 96).

que ferais-je sans ce monde sans visage sans questions
Time of writing and publication as above. In the first line *visage* was originally plural. In line 10 the wording was originally *comme hier comme avant-hier*.

je voudrais que mon amour meure
Date of writing and publication as above. Variation in the French version in line 3 from *et dans les rues* and in line 4 from *pleurant la seule qui m'ait aimé*. In the English section the last line originally read *mourning the first and last to love me (Poems in English,* John Calder, London 1961), but was varied in later editions with an alternative last line *mourning her who sought to love me.* The last line has now been finally changed to *mourning her who thought she loved me.* The lady in question is often assumed to have been Lucia Joyce.

être là sans mâchoires sans dents
Written between 1937 and 1939 and appeared for the first time in *Les Temps Modernes* (as above).

Ascension
Same as above.

La Mouche
Same as above. Compare with the last verse of *Serena I* in Part One.

musique de l'indifférence
This poem also appeared during the same period and was first published in *Les Temps Modernes* (as above).

bois seul
Same as above.

ainsi a-t-on beau
Same as above. In line 11 *bon* was originally *gentil.*

Rue de Vaugirard
Same as above. Line 2 originally started *je me débraye.*

Dieppe
Written in 1937 and suggested by a passage from *Der Spaziergang* by Hölderlin. First appeared in *Les Temps Modernes* (as above). Last line now changed from *towards the lighted town.*

Arènes de Lutèce
Same as above. Line 21 was originally *qui vous éclaire.*

The Notes to Part Two are translated from those prepared by John Fletcher for Editions de Minuit (1968) and revised by the publishers.

Mirlitonnades (Bird Calls). The author says 'written spasmodically on scraps of paper. Nothing dated.' Thirty-five of them, written in French, were first published by Les Editions de Minuit in 1978, dated 1976–1978. Other have been found in the Beckett Archive at Reading University (See *Late Poems*, above).

Comment dire. What is the word.
This, written in French and then translated into English, was Samuel Beckett's final written work. Although his brain was perfectly clear he had difficulty in remembering names and increasingly finding the word that he needed or being able to spell it, which on occasion might be for a crossword puzzle.

PART THREE

No Sighs for Sale
First appeared in a collection of Poems by André Bosquet, published in New York, and then in an Irish collection in 1988. It was picked up by Poems in the Underground in London, which led to its present inclusion.

Translations from Eluard
These appeared together with many other translations by Samuel Beckett in the special Surrealist Number of *This Quarter* (Guest Editor: André Breton) in September 1932. The poems come from four collections: *Mourir de ne pas Mourir, La Vie immédiate, L' Amour la poésie,* and *A Toute Epreuve.*

Drunken Boat
The circumstances in which Samuel Beckett's early unpublished translation of Arthur Rimbaud's *Le Bateau ivre* came to be written are in themselves of some interest. But the reasons why his original typescript has been preserved and the coincidence that led to its eventual publication, more than fifty years after it was written, are even more curious and worth relating.

At the end of December 1931, Beckett left Trinity College, Dublin, where he had been Lecturer in French for only four terms. He then travelled to Germany and resigned his academic appointment by post from Kassel. After a short stay in Germany, he moved to Paris where he joined his friend and fellow Irishman, Thomas MacGreevy, with whom Beckett had been *lecteur d'anglais* at the École Normale Superiéure in the rue d'Ulm in 1928, Beckett staying on alone for a further year. It was in 1932, while staying in the same hotel as MacGreevy, that Beckett was working on his first unpublished novel, *Dream of fair to middling women.*

Following the assassination of the President of the Republic, Paul Doumer, on 7 May 1932 by the White Russian, Gorguloff, it was decided that a check should be made on the papers of all foreigners who were then living in Paris. Since Beckett did not possess a valid *carte de séjour,* he was forced to leave his hotel, and, as he could not legitimately register elsewhere, he spent several nights sleeping on the floor in the Studio Villa Seurat of the painter, Jean Lurçat. In order to obtain money to leave the country, Beckett called on Edward Titus, the editor of the literary review, *This Quarter,* at his offices in the rue Delambre. Earlier, Titus had expressed interest in publishing an English translation of Rimbaud's poem, *Le Bateau ivre,* and it was with this in mind that Beckett now completed a translation of the poem, begun by him some time before. He had already produced several translations from the Italian of Montale, Franchi, and Comisso, which Titus had published in *This Quarter* in 1930; a little later he had translated poems and prose by Breton, Éluard and Crevel for the special number on Surrealism which was to appear, edited by André Breton, in September 1932. Beckett had accepted this earlier work as a paid commission and, in view of his difficult financial situation, he asked Titus for a thousand francs for *Drunken Boat*. In the event, he was offered seven hundred francs for the poem, which allowed him to travel to London and live there for a short time, near the Gray's Inn Road. It was during this stay in London that Beckett tried to organise for himself a career in literary journalism, but a call on Desmond McCarthy failed to bring the commissioned reviewing that he had hoped for. Soon after this the money paid to him by Titus ran out and Beckett was forced to return home to Dublin where he could stay for nothing in the family house in Foxrock. The following year his father died, leaving Samuel, his second son, a small annuity, intended as the equivalent of his share in the family business, which was continued by his brother, Frank Edward. The money enabled Beckett to travel further in Europe and eventually allowed him to settle in Paris in 1937.

It was Beckett's custom to type out three copies of anything that he wrote and there is no reason to suppose that he acted differently with the translation, *Drunken Boat*. Nothing is known as to the whereabouts of Titus's typed copy nor of the reasons for his failure to publish the poem in *This Quarter*. The review continued however, only until the end of 1932, when publication was discontinued. Similarly, there is no trace of the original manuscript or of the third copy. The top copy of the text was, however, given by Beckett in the mid 1930s to an Irish friend, Nuala Costello, in whose private library it has been kept until 1976. It was while he was on a fox-hunting holiday in Ireland that my co-editor, Felix Leakey, met, quite by chance, the owner of the typescript and spoke to her of the Samuel Beckett collection in Reading University Library. She recalled that Beckett had gifted to her an early work that might well interest me as the founder of the Beckett Archive. This proved to be the typescript of the unpublished 'spoof' lecture which Beckett had given to the Modern Language Society at Trinity College, Dublin. This lecture, which is referred to in the Beckett bibliography by Raymond Federman and John Fletcher, *Samuel Beckett: his works and his critics*, as 'probably lost', is about an imaginary literary movement in France, entitled not as had been thought 'Le Convergisme' but 'Le Concentrisme', whose exponent is said to be one Jean du Chas, the author of a 'Discours de la Sortie'; the lecture is clever and extremely funny. This typescript, with some manuscript corrections in Beckett's hand, is now on permanent loan to Reading University Library. On a second visit to Ireland by Felix Leakey, the owner of 'Le Concentrisme' produced for him the typescript of another early piece by Beckett, also described in the Beckett bibliography as 'probably lost'. This was the present translation by Beckett of Rimbaud's *Le Bateau ivre*. The preservation of the typescript of *Drunken Boat* is even more surprising, since it survived a fire in the owner's house only because it had been folded away

223

in her copy of *The Oxford Book of French Verse*, between the pages in which the original Rimbaud poem is printed. As the facsimile reproduction reveals, the pages of Beckett's typescript have been charred by fire. It is therefore as a result of a series of coincidences that Beckett's translation has found its way into the Beckett collection in Reading and that, thanks to the kindness of its owner and Samuel Beckett, we can publish the text.

This note on the circumstances of composition and publication first appeared in the De Luxe edition of the poem and its translation published by Whiteknights Press 1976 and was written by James Knowlson to whom the publishers are greatly indebted for this and other assistance in preparing the third and the present edition, now slightly updated.

Zone
This translation first appeared in *Transition 50*, a post-war issue edited by Georges Duthuit in October 1950. It was republished in 1972 by Dolmen Press, Dublin in association with Calder and Boyars.

Adaptations from Chamfort
The first six maxims appeared in *The Blue Guitar*, Facoltà di Magistero, Università degli Studi di Messina, Volume I, No. 1 in December 1975, and the last two were written in 1976 while the last edition was in preparation.

PART FOUR

This section of juvenilia consists of poems written as a very young man, and exhibit the erudition of a brilliant scholar, deeply influenced by the Italian and French poets he had studied at Trinity, but unable to escape from the influence of T.S. Eliot (particularily Eliot's *Waste Land*). The poems are deeply intertwined with his first prose experiments, especially *Dream of Fair to middling Women*, written in 1932, but only published posthumously in 1993. They also reflect other preoccupation of Beckett at the time, especially his *amours*. All the poems in this section, although 'jetissoned' by their author, appeared, in a discontinuous form, in Laurence Harvey's ground-breaking analytical examination of his work, *Samuel Beckett: Poet and Critic* (Princeton University Press 1970).

Calvary by Night
This also first appears in *Dream*, and shows an early concern with the image of life as a brief flowering between birth and death that occurs throughout his work.

Casket of Pralinen For A Daughter Of A Dissipated Mandarin
Harvey comments that this poem relies heavily on Beaumarchais, the Bible, Dahlberg (the German painter), Proust, Wordsworth and others. It was probably written shortly after leaving Trinity.

Sonnet
This can be found in *Dream of Fair to middling Women* as a sonnet to the hero's love of the moment, the Smeraldina, and is in part a parody.

Text
'Leans heavily on Proust, the mythology of Tiresias, the Bible and Dante' says Harvey. The stylistic similarity to *Whoroscope*, his first published poem (1930) is evident.

For Future Reference
Many autobiographical references occur in this poem, including his fascination since childhood with diving into water from a height, the cause of early terror when pushed to do so by his father.

Hell Crane to Starling
Harvey comments: 'The personal element (more a lecherous leer than the recalled emotion of authentic experience) is all but submerged by the Biblical and Dantesque materials.' Tsoar in *Genesis* is where Lot retired to a cave while God was pouring fire and brimstone on Sodom and Gomorrah.

225

While staying in the city where free love and easy conquest was common, Beckett, as a normal young man, was at this time particularly aware of the conflict existing between the desire to satisfy natural feelings of lust, and the guilt inherited from the puritanical Ireland that he had just left. Harvey comments further: 'Eroticism may offer a corrective to Irish Puritanism, but it has its own dangers. It can lead to carnal enslavement, boredom (see *elles viennent*) or to paralysed or even marital commitment.'

From The Only Poet To A Shining Whore
There are references here to Dante and the Bible. Rahab, the harlot of Jericho and Dante's love, Beatrice, both figure in the poem. Henry Crowder was a black American pianist, the lover of Nancy Cunard, whom Beckett met in his early Paris years and the poem was written at the instigation of Cunard and much appreciated by Crowder at the time.

Return To The Vestry
This poem is heavily influenced by Ronsard (*Magie, ou delivrance d'amour* is quoted here), both by the work and life of a man who believed his work would be immortal and ended up in minor orders in the church. There are references to the chapel in which Ronsard is believed to be buried.

Yoke of Liberty
The title comes from Dante. Beckett's equal and conflicting need, to be alone and to love, are illustrated here.

Tailpiece
This poem was originally an addendum to the novel *Watt*, first published in 1953, and was included as a tailpiece or envoi by the author in the last collected edition, and once again in the present one.

In addition to those mentioned above, and Editions de Minuit, publishers of the poems written in French, the publishers wish to acknowledge the editorial work done by Sheila O'Leary in preparing the present volume.

They are also grateful to the Beckett Archive at Reading University for access to unpublished work.